Walt Disney's

MICKEY MOUSE

HIS LIFE AND TIMES

Walt Disney's MICKEY MOUSE

HIS LIFE AND TIMES

1817

HARPER & ROW, PUBLISHERS, New York

Cambridge, Philadelphia, San Francisco, London
Mexico City, São Paulo, Singapore, Sydney

ACKNOWLEDGEMENTS

It seems somehow appropriate that Mickey Mouse, with his innate good-manners, should wait until the official biographies of Goofy and Donald had been published before allowing his own story to appear in print. Here at last, however, is *Mickey Mouse: His Life and Times,* the third in the series that began with *Donald Duck: 50 Years of Happy Frustration* and *Goofy: The Good Sport.*

This series could not have existed without the close co-operation and support of the Walt Disney Company, especially the Archive department. Our thanks to Keith Bales, Bo Boyd, David Cleghorn, Greg Crosby, Wendall Mohler, Wayne Morris, Rose Motzko, Paula Sigman and David R. Smith.

Special thanks are due also to the team who produced the book, particularly Richard Hollis and Brian Sibley, who provided research and the text, and to Malcolm Couch and Leslie Posner.

Our thanks, too, to the publishers who simultaneously committed themselves to the project: Hachette in France, Harper & Row in the United States, IPC in Britain and Loeb in the Netherlands.

I trust that some of the fun that we have had while working on this book is reflected in the pages that follow and that you, like us, will enjoy the story of Mickey's life and times!

Justin Knowles

Richard Holliss and Brian Sibley express their gratitude to Robin Allan, Brian Beacock, Peter Halsey and Muir Hewitt for their generous help and advice; to Brenda Ford for her assistance with typing the manuscript; and to their long-suffering loved ones for their patient support.

R.H. and B.S.

Library of Congress Cataloging in Publication Data

Holliss, Richard
    Walt Disney's Mickey Mouse
Filmography: p.
Bibliography: p.
1. Mickey Mouse (cartoon character) in mass media.
I. Sibley, Brian.   II. Title.   III. Title: Mickey Mouse
P96.M53H6   1986   741.5'09794'93   86-45115
ISBN 0-06-015619-8
ISBN 0-06-091402-5 (paperback)

© The Walt Disney Company 1986

Published simultaneously in Canada by
Fitzhenry & Whiteside Limited, Toronto

First U.S. edition

Produced by the Justin Knowles Publishing Group
9 Colleton Crescent, Exeter, Devon EX2 4BY, UK

Text and research: Richard Holliss and Brian Sibley
Additional research: Leslie Posner
Design: Malcolm Couch
Production: Nick Facer

CONTENTS

INTRODUCTION 6

THE BIRTH OF A MOUSE NAMED MICKEY 8

OF MOUSE AND MEN
MOUSE MYTHS AND MOUSE FACTS

MICKEY IN HOLLYWOOD 16

THE MOUSE SPEAKS
FROM BLACK AND WHITE TO COLOUR
INTERNATIONAL MOVIE-STAR

THE WORLD OF MICKEY MOUSE 28

COUNTRY MOUSE AND TOWN MOUSE
MICKEY AND MINNIE: A FINE ROMANCE
FRIENDS AND FOES

MAKING MICKEY MOVE 40

EARLY ANATOMY – CIRCLES AND RUBBER HOSES
THE MOUSE EVOLVES

MOUSE OF A THOUSAND FACES 46

AT WORK AND PLAY
HERO AND ADVENTURER
IN STRANGE LANDS AND OTHER WORLDS
SONG-AND-DANCE MOUSE

MICKEY'S WAR AND AFTER 60

MICKEY'S GREATEST PERFORMANCE
MICKEY DOES HIS BIT
FUN AND FROLICS

MOUSEMANIA 72

MARKETING THE MOUSE
MOUSE BOOKS AND COMICS
WHO'S THE LEADER OF THE CLUB?

MICKEY'S NEW LEASE OF LIFE 84

THE HOST WITH THE MOST
MODERN MOUSE
BACK IN FRONT OF THE CAMERA

BIBLIOGRAPHY 95

FILMOGRAPHY 96

INTRODUCTION

There is no doubt about it, Mickey Mouse is the most universally known and loved cartoon character ever created.

Bright-eyed, innocent, ever-hopeful and courageous, his beaming smile and open-handed gesture of welcome signify warmth and friendliness to people all over the world – from Alaska to Zanzibar – and have done so now for almost sixty years.

Mickey Mouse has acted in over 130 movies, appeared on stage and television, has made records and videos and been featured in books and comics, as well as decorating a veritable department store of merchandise from mass-produced 10-cent toys to exclusively made thousand-dollar jewellery.

This impudent little scrap of a character entered the world on 18 November 1928, in a film called *Steamboat Willie*, which just happened to be the cinema's first ever talking cartoon. By 1930, Mickey had his own entry in Hollywood's directory of actors – "Height: 2' 3", Weight: 23 pounds, Agent: Walt Disney" – and he was being ranked alongside Charlie Chaplin and Greta Garbo as one of the all-time movie greats.

"Perhaps it is one of the many paradoxes of the picture business," wrote Walt Disney in 1934, "that a star who has taken the screen by storm should receive no salary for his services, and should have been made not born. His exploits have brought in many thousands of pounds, though the star himself is just something out of an ink-pot."

Despite those inky origins, Mickey won as many admirers as any flesh-and-blood star has ever done. Kings, presidents, princes and dictators numbered themselves among his fans, men of letters acclaimed him and popular song-writers sang his praises. In 1934, for example, the great Cole Porter included the line "You're Mickey Mouse" in his hit song "You're the Top".

Kids joined Mickey Mouse Clubs in their millions, a Hollywood gossip-writer penned a monthly column called "Mickey Mouse's Diary," and Mickey found himself listed in the *Encyclopaedia Britannica* and having his portrait hung in the fashionable art galleries of London and New York.

So potent and powerful a character was Mickey that a witchdoctor in the Belgian Congo reputedly used a home-made mask of "Mikimus" to give his *voo* a little extra *do*.

Mickey was pondered by pundits and analysed by psychologists, who observed that his head comprised a trinity of circles and that the circle, as philosopher Carl Jung

had said, "always points to the single most vital aspect of life – its ultimate wholeness."

Ordinary film-goers, who knew nothing about Jung, simply liked Mickey Mouse because he made them laugh. One woman claimed that a persistent attack of hiccups had been cured through laughing at a Mickey Mouse cartoon; another discovered her long-lost brother when she recognized his laugh in a darkened movie-theatre. And a gentleman once wrote to Disney asking for a contribution to the hospital bill he had incurred as a result of a case of appendicitis brought on by laughing too much at Mickey.

Mickey is all things to all men – a reflection, perhaps, of the diversity of roles he has played over the years: farm-boy, taxi-driver, fireman, car-mechanic, store-keeper, building-worker and tug-boat skipper.

He has acted in comedies, melodramas and historical epics; his love of music, song and dance has been demonstrated in dozens of virtuoso performances and led to his conducting everything from ragtime to grand opera. In his greatest performance, as the Sorcerer's Apprentice in *Fantasia*, Mickey gave the most compelling popular interpretation of classical music ever seen in the movies.

Writing in *The Art of Walt Disney* in 1942, Robert D. Feild asked: "What is Mickey anyway but an abstract idea in the process of becoming?" And that is what Mickey has always been – adapting his style to suit the ever-changing times: from the years of the Depression to those of revival and expansion; from the jazz age to the space age.

In order to do this, Mickey has also had to adapt to the changes and developments within the entertainment industry. He made his début at the same time as the talkies; later, he experimented with colour and stereo sound. In the 1950s, he went into television and the theme-park business, helping Walt Disney expand his film Studio into a huge corporation. It was, as Disney once remarked, not so much a case of "a house that Jack built, but a castle a Mouse built."

Being an incomparable showman, Mickey took pride in discovering and introducing to the world a galaxy of other stars, including the ever-winsome Minnie Mouse, the lovable Pluto, the accident-prone Goofy and the irascible Donald Duck. Some of these characters challenged Mickey's popularity, but they could never truly supplant him. For Mickey has always been something very special – a symbol of optimism, fun and joy.

It is hoped that this long-overdue appreciation of Mickey's life and times will provide an insight into the mystique and enduring appeal of this Mouse for all Seasons.

Richard Holliss

Brian Sibley

THE BIRTH OF A MOUSE NAMED MICKEY

OF MOUSE AND MEN

Walt Disney was often referred to as Mickey Mouse's father, but Mickey actually had *two* fathers: Walt Disney and Ub Iwerks.

Both men were born in 1901: Ub Iwerks on 24 March in Kansas City; Walt Disney on 5 December in Chicago. Walt's full name was Walter Elias Disney; Ub Iwerks, whose father was Dutch, was christened Ubbe Ert Iwwerks, but not long after he met Walt, he simplified his name to Ub Iwerks. Walt, however, was still calling himself Walter E. Disney.

The young Disney had moved to Kansas City with his family (via a farm in Missouri) in 1910, and it was there, nine years later, that he met Iwerks. Both were 17 years old and working as artists for the Pesmen-Rubin Commercial Art Studio. They soon became close friends and, the following year, decided to set up in business together.

Calling themselves "Iwerks-Disney" (because, Walt said, "Disney-Iwerks" sounded like a firm of opticians), they produced drawings and lettering for such august publications as *The United Leather Workers' Journal* and *The Restaurant News*.

The Iwerks-Disney studio survived only a few weeks however, for Walt successfully applied for a job with the Kansas City Slide Company. Ub joined him shortly afterwards, and it proved an important step in both men's careers, as it was there that they learned the rudiments of film animation and were captivated by the idea of making drawings move.

Walt Disney was always a man of vision and enterprise, and in 1922 he started his own animation studio called Laugh-o-Gram Films, Inc. He enlisted Iwerks, who soon established himself as Disney's most valuable artistic asset.

When, the following year, the company went bankrupt, Iwerks returned to the Kansas City Slide Company (now called the United Film Ad Company), while Disney took off for Hollywood in search of a job and hoping to find a distributor for their most recent film, *Alice's Wonderland*, featuring the adventures of a live child actress in a world of cartoon animals – including some primitive forerunners of Mickey Mouse.

Disney sold the idea for a series to Miss M.J. Winkler. His older brother, Roy, offered $250 and, together with another $500 from their Uncle Robert, they rented a studio and hired a couple of ink and paint girls, one of whom – Lillian Bounds – became Walt's wife.

Disney animated the first six *Alice* films by himself. However, he was soon in need of assistance and, in May 1924, sent for his old friend Iwerks. Two months later, Ub was in Hollywood working on more *Alice* films and, from 1927, on a series featuring a new cartoon character called Oswald the Lucky Rabbit.

Oswald didn't quite live up to his name, and, early in 1928, Disney discovered that his star was actually the property of Universal, and Charles Mintz, who had married Miss Winkler, was now running her company. He also found that Mintz had signed up all of his animators – with the exception of Ub Iwerks.

A new character had to be invented, and Mickey Mouse was born, with Ub Iwerks assisting at the birth.

The idea for Mickey was Disney's: he dictated the Mouse's character and personality, supplied his voice and devised and wrote his earliest film scripts. But the visual realization of the character was the work of Ub Iwerks.

Iwerks was well paid – his starting salary in Hollywood had been $40 a week (which was more than Disney paid himself)

Walt and Mickey celebrate the winning of a special Oscar in 1932 by posing for a photograph with the Studio staff. On Walt's right is his brother, Roy; kneeling in front of Roy is Floyd Gottfredson, who drew Mickey's comic-strip adventures, and kneeling on Mickey's left is animator Les Clark.

Ub Iwerks, photographed around the time of Mickey's début in 1928.

and had risen to $120 a week. But he worked hard for his money. Iwerks' ability as an animator became legendary within the industry; he was not only a gifted draughtsman he was also a prolific one.

An experienced animator can produce between 80 and 100 drawings a week, but Iwerks produced 700 drawings – in one day! "I've always had a competitive nature," he once recalled, "I'd heard that Bill Nolan, who was doing 'Krazy Kat', had done five hundred or six hundred drawings a day, so I really extended myself."

Iwerks certainly extended himself in producing the early Mickey Mouse films. The first to be made (but third released) was *Plane Crazy*, and Iwerks animated the film on his own in under three weeks. He was also largely responsible for Mickey's next two movies, *Gallopin' Gaucho* and *Steamboat Willie*, although he was assisted by Les Clark, an animator whom Disney had hired in 1927.

"You know this is only a temporary job, Les," Disney had told the young artist, "I don't know what's going to happen."

What happened was that *Steamboat Willie* became the cinema's first synchronized sound cartoon and Mickey Mouse became one of the biggest stars in filmland, and – 48 years later – Les Clark was still working at the Disney Studio.

As well as producing much of the animation for Mickey's early films, Iwerks also drew all the backgrounds and designed posters for the movies, and in acknowledgement of his contribution, Disney shared billing with him. The opening credits for *Steamboat Willie* read "A Walt Disney Comic by Ub Iwerks."

Their names also appeared jointly on the first Mickey Mouse newspaper comic strips, which began in January 1930 and were written by Disney and drawn by Iwerks. Later that month, Iwerks left to establish his own studio, producing many cartoon shorts for other distributors and creating his own animated characters, Flip the Frog, and Willie Whopper, before returning to the Disney Studio in 1940, where he worked until his death in 1971.

Over the years, as Walt Disney became increasingly busy with the many activities of his expanding studio, a number of other artists began to have a hand in Mickey's career. Among those who became, as it were, step-fathers to the Mouse were Wilfred Jackson, Les Clark, Frank Thomas, Ward Kimball, Preston Blair and an artist

Mickey's spirit of adventure was soon established when, in *Plane Crazy* (1928), he and Minnie headed off into the bright blue yonder; and his reputation for clowning around began in *Steamboat Willie* (also 1928), in which he enjoyed himself as a one-mouse band.

However, there was more to their relationship than shared vocal chords; something of Walt's character had been passed on to the Mouse.

Irving Wallace, writing in *Collier's* in 1949, quoted one of Disney's animators who had noticed that Walt and Mickey had "the same soulful eyes, the same beaky face, the same trick of falling into pantomime when at a loss for words."

Les Clark worked on the early Mickey Mouse films, including *Steamboat Willie*. Although hired on a "temporary" basis, Clark continued to work at the Studio until his retirement in 1976.

who did much to shape Mickey's later screen appearance – Fred Moore.

"Fred Moore," says animator Marc Davis, "*was* Disney drawing. We've all done things on our own, but that was the basis of what Disney stood for. It was certainly the springboard for everything that came after."

If Fred Moore's animation symbolized the Disney style, then Mickey certainly symbolized Disney. The character of the Mouse, alone among all the Studio's creations, became and remained forever associated with Walt Disney.

Indeed, Walt had provided Mickey's fluting falsetto from 1928 until 1946 when the role was assumed by studio sound-effects man, Jimmy Macdonald. Commenting on Disney's mouse-voice, biographer Bob Thomas remarked: "It is no easy matter to get color into such an unnatural, limited voice, but Walt managed. No one else could capture the gulping, ingenuous, half-brave quality."

But the likeness between man and mouse was more than just skin-deep. "Both Walt and Mickey," wrote Bob Thomas, "had an adventurous spirit, a sense of rectitude, an admitted lack of sophistication, a boyish ambition to excel. . . . The Disney animators recognized this unstated similarity, and when drawing the Mouse often kept in mind – subconsciously, at least – the characteristics of Walt."

Helped along by the romantic interpretations of various journalists, the legend that Mickey was Walt's *alter ego* (or vice versa) became a fact.

Only Mrs. Disney, it seems, remained unconvinced. In a rare interview, with *McCall's Magazine* in 1953, Walt's wife assured Isabella Taves that "Father is no mouse. Walt was the first voice of Mickey Mouse. Because of that, and because Walt can seem shy and retiring with people he doesn't know, and because Roy has been heard to complain that Walt has no more money sense than Mickey Mouse, the myth has grown up that Mickey Mouse is a projection of Walt's real personality. I can assure you it isn't true. No matter how hard the rest of us squeal, Walt goes ahead and does what he wants to do."

And an anonymous Disney animator told Hedda Hopper that "sometimes when you go into his office expecting to meet Mickey Mouse, you find Donald Duck instead."

Walt Disney himself was content to admit the likeness between himself and his Mouse, and remained forever loyal to his little friend – giving him new opportunities for work and retaining him as the symbol of the entire Disney corporation. "Mickey and I are firm friends," Disney told the *Windsor* magazine in January 1934. "We have weathered the storms together. I have tried to give him a soul and a 'keep kissable' disposition."

Writing of Disney in London's *Sunday Dispatch* in 1960, Herbert Kretzmer said: "He is a 60 year old child, with a child's uncontaminated sense of innocence and astonishment . . . a child's natural sympathy with the living things of the world." To that extent, if to no other, man and mouse were as one.

And, although Walt Disney died on 15 December 1966, there is a sense in which he still lives on in the person of Mickey Mouse.

MOUSE MYTHS AND MOUSE FACTS

The birth of Mickey Mouse is as exciting a story as that of his creator Walt Disney's road to success. But how did that popular little mouse with the large black ears come into being? According to a *Mickey Mouse Annual* in 1945, in a story entitled *Redskin Raiders,* it all began a long time ago, "long before Mr. Walt Disney ever made film stars of Mickey Mouse and the gang: long before we ever heard of them in fact! In those days Mickey Mouse was a bright young lad helping his Uncle with his grocery store and eating house, in the tiny town of Largeville in the Middle West." Mickey would probably confirm such a wonderful story as his early life was certainly full of adventure.

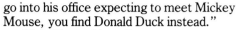

He has, of course, been interviewed in numerous magazines, remarking on one occasion that he even remembered Oswald the Lucky Rabbit: "he was working for Walt about the time I was starting out," he told a reporter for *Funnyworld*. "He decided to quit and go over to Walter Lantz . . . Now where is Oswald the Rabbit today? There's a new generation that's never heard of him."

In 1930, a Mickey Mouse book published by the firm of Bibo and Lang, claimed it knew the origin of Mickey. Eleven-year-old writer Bobette Bibo described how Mickey was actually mouse number 13 in Mouse Fairyland but was kicked out by the King for constantly playing pranks on the royal person. He was kicked a long way for he finally found himself in Hollywood, where he met Walt Disney. Unlike the King, Walt liked his playful manner. "'You give me an idea for a series of comedies. I have an idea that I can make you a picture star . . . but first of all,

we shall have to get you another name. Come sit up here on the desk. What did you do when you first came to my house?' 'I ate old green cheese' said the mouse promptly – 'Now let me see; green is the colour of Ireland,' said Mr. Disney, musingly, 'Green, Irish, Mickey! I have it! Mickey Mouse shall be your name!'"

Over the years, interviews with Walt Disney hinted at a variety of possible explanations behind Mickey's birth. In the *Minneapolis Star*, in 1933, Walt said, "I got the idea, I suppose, when I was working in an office in Kansas City. The girls used to put their lunches in wire waste baskets and everyday the mice would scamper around in them after crumbs. I got interested and began collecting a family in an old box. They became very tame and by the time I was ready to turn them loose they were so friendly they just sat there on the floor looking at me."

Other stories recount how Disney trained one mouse in particular to sit on his

Mickey refused to be intimidated by the imposing figure of steamboat Captain Pete. *Steamboat Willie*, made in 1928, was Mickey's screen début.

Walt Disney pictured outside the entrance to his Hyperion Avenue Studio with the stars of his one-reel *Alice* comedies. Margie Gay had, by this time, replaced the original "Alice", Virginia Davis.

drawing board and eat scraps of food. Whatever the truth, one thing is certain, Walt didn't call any of his pet mice "Mickey" – at least not yet. *Cosmopolitan* in 1934 argued that "mice on the drawing board" was completely untrue and that they had it on good authority that "Mickey Mouse's papa is not overly fond of mice. He jumps out of their way, and doesn't go looking for them." In fact, Walt later admitted, "I had this mouse in the back of my head . . . because a mouse is sort of a sympathetic character in spite of the fact that everybody's frightened of a mouse . . . including myself."

The truth about Mickey's creation is that he was invented when, in 1928, Disney lost the rights to his character Oswald the Lucky Rabbit.

Following a disastrous meeting with his distributor in New York, Walt and his wife Lillian boarded a train back to Hollywood. His mood was despairing, he had a small studio on Hyperion Avenue, hardly anything in the bank, and nothing to animate. It was to be a historic journey. As the train trundled westward, Walt, legend has it, sat and scribbled all kinds of new animals on his drawing pad. Finally, he came up with a mouse. Excitedly he referred to his creation as "Mortimer Mouse," but Lillian didn't like the sound of it, as she told Isabella Taves in *McCalls*: "'Mortimer* is a horrible name for a mouse!' I exclaimed. Walt argued – he can be very persuasive – but I stood firm. Finally to placate his stubborn wife, Walt came up with a substitute: *Mickey Mouse*."

Variations on this story have been printed in numerous publications. According to W. T. Maxwell in the *Daily Sketch* (1938), Disney was trying to get to sleep in the upper berth of the Hollywood-bound train when, "the continuous but slight creaking of the woodwork in his compartment sounded like a million mice in conference. The idea

made him laugh and in that split second Mickey Mouse was born."

In "The Life Story of Mickey Mouse," Walt remembered how the idea of a mouse completely engulfed him. "The wheels turned to the tune of it – 'chug, chug mouse, chug, chug mouse,' the train seemed to say – The whistle screeched it. 'A m-m-m owa-ouse' it wailed. By the time my train had reached the Middle West I had dressed my dream mouse in a pair of red velvet pants with two huge pearl buttons, had composed the first scenario, and was all set."

In an interview with the Studio, Mickey told a slightly different story. "Destiny brought us together. We shared the same seat on the train. Having heard from my cousins in Kansas City that Mr. Disney was good to his pet mice as a boy, I volunteered my services as a cartoon character. After we got to Hollywood, Mr. Disney made a few sketches of me and gave me a screen test." Poor Lillian doesn't even get the credit for changing the mouse's name. Disney adds that the character remained "Mortimer" until a film producer, who laughed loudly at the suggestion, persuaded the young animator to rename him "Mickey." It may also have alarmed the railroad company, if they had discovered that it was actually a real mouse Walt met on the train.

A more accurate account was probably that of Iwerks, the one animator responsible for drawing the early Mickey Mouse cartoons, who later recalled in an interview that Mickey was eventually thought up at an animators' meeting in Hollywood shortly after Disney returned from New York.

In one interview Walt even went as far as giving the credit for Mickey's creation to his idol Charlie Chaplin. "We wanted something appealing and we thought of a tiny bit of a mouse that would have something of the wistfulness of Chaplin – a little fellow trying to do the best he could."

Whatever the real truth behind Mickey's origins, it was only a step towards a greater goal. For the little mouse, with such a secretive background, was destined for real stardom and was about to put Walt Disney's small animation company on the map.

Walt Disney, photographed during the 1950s with one of the first Mickey Mouse dolls made some 20 years earlier.

MICKEY IN HOLLYWOOD
THE MOUSE SPEAKS

It may be true that Walt Disney created Mickey Mouse on a train journey back from New York, but what isn't clear is whether the scenario for the first Mickey film, *Plane Crazy* (1928), was also decided upon during that fateful trip. According to some sources, Mickey's screen début was planned at a Hollywood story conference with animator Ub Iwerks. In 1927, Charles Lindbergh had made newspaper headlines around the world for his historic solo flight from New York to Paris. It seemed natural, therefore, to a cartoonist like Disney to spoof the nation's admiration for Lindburgh.

In *Plane Crazy,* Mickey, helped by his farmyard friends, built his own plane. While looking through the flight manual, he came across a picture of his hero. Ruffling his hair in order to imitate Lindbergh's dashing looks, Mickey took to the air. When the flight ended in disaster, Mickey transformed his car into another aircraft and took Minnie for a spin, but an incident with a cow eventually brought both mice down to earth with a bump.

Film critic Richard Schickel later noted that "the film is not a bad piece of animation when judged by the standards of its time. Particularly, in the anthropomorphizing of inanimate objects, like the airplane in which Mickey takes Minnie up for the ride, it is quite good."

In order to finish the film as quickly as possible, Walt set up a makeshift studio at his home on Lyric Avenue. Walt's wife, Lillian, and Roy's wife, Edna, inked and painted the cels from Iwerks' drawings. Some of Disney's animators had been signed up by Charles Mintz, and, anxious that these men should not find out about Mickey Mouse, Disney insisted that Iwerks worked alone. To keep the project secret, *Plane Crazy* was shot at the studio after hours by cameraman Mike Marcus. When completed, it was given a special preview at a Sunset Boulevard movie-house on 15 May 1928. As it was well received, Walt gave the go-ahead for a second Mickey Mouse film, *Gallopin' Gaucho*. Ready for a screening in August of the same year,

Mickey proved that he was just "plane crazy" over Minnie when he took her flying in their first film together in 1928.

Gallopin' Gaucho relates how Mickey saved Minnie in a South American backwater from the evil clutches of Pete. Unfortunately for Disney, the New York exhibitors weren't too enthusiastic, but, undaunted by their lukewarm response, Disney ordered work to begin on a third Mickey Mouse film, *Steamboat Willie*.

But a revolution was about to take place in Hollywood, one that would affect Disney's whole outlook – Warner Brothers released the first talking picture, *The Jazz Singer*. Excited by the possibilities of sound film, Disney realized that his Mickey Mouse cartoons needed a soundtrack, but he had no clear idea what was required to produce sound on film. Animator Wilfred Jackson, who had recently joined the studio, worked alongside Disney in devising a system for synchronizing sound: "I played the harmonica so that Walt could tell the tempo that he wanted for 'Steamboat Bill' and 'Turkey in the Straw' [the two main songs chosen for the film]." Jackson bought a metronome: "Walt knew how fast film went (ninety feet a minute), and I knew about the metronome. Putting the two together made it possible to pre-time music to animation when the music would be recorded later just by simple mathematics." The metronome measured their rhythm. As Jackson remembered, "Walt made up the exposure sheet for 'Willie'. What I worked out was a bar sheet or dope sheet, to indicate measures of music." Jackson adds that this wasn't actually a score, but rather a kind of sophisticated storyboard. "It had a little square for each beat in each measure and it had an indication of the tempo; it was in twelve frames, or sixteen frames, or whatever, to the beat . . . within that square, the key action and the scene number was indicated."

In *Steamboat Willie* Mickey played a member of Captain Pete's riverboat crew, who entertained the ship's only passenger, Minnie Mouse, with a rendition of "Turkey in the Straw". To provide the music, Mickey squeezed, hammered and half-strangled the animals aboard the boat, even using a cow's teeth as a xylophone. Despite underlining the cruelty of some early animated films, this episode proved to be the highlight of the movie. As Richard Schickel pointed out in his biography of Disney, "even today the effect of the sequence is catchy, in 1928 it must have been truly stunning."

In order to test its effect on an audience, Disney ran the completed film of *Steamboat Willie* on a large bedsheet over the studio doorway for members of his family. Behind the screen, but situated so they could see the action, Disney, Iwerks and Jackson played a multitude of musical objects from cowbells and whistles to rubber plungers and pop-guns. Their wives weren't very impressed by what they saw, but Disney realized its potential. However, he also knew that getting the soundtrack synchronized to the film wasn't going to be

Although *Steamboat Willie* (1928) was Disney's first "talkie," Mickey didn't actually speak. The film was full of an incredible number of growls, whines and squeaks.

easy, and he contacted an organist friend, Carl Stalling, in Kansas City. Stalling agreed to write a score for the film, timed to the animator's exposure sheet.

With a print of *Steamboat Willie* and Stalling's score, Disney visited every sound-recording studio in New York, but to no avail. Eventually he found a company called Cinephone headed by Pat Powers, who agreed to record sound on to the picture. But getting the recording synchronized proved not only expensive but difficult. In order to aid the conductor, Carl Edouarde, the bandleader of the Broadway Strand, in timing the sound effects exactly, rumour has it that Disney added a spot of india ink to every twelfth frame so that a flash appeared on screen every half second. Following these flashes with beats of music, the orchestra kept in perfect synchronization with the film. Walt himself provided Mickey's squeaks and the voice of a parrot calling out "Man overboard!"

Steamboat Willie opened at the Colony Theatre in New York on 18 November 1928 to tremendous acclaim. The press were ecstatic: "I want to thank Mr. Walter Disney for giving me a laugh, one of the best I've had in a motion picture theatre for quite some time," said the *Exhibitor's Herald. Variety* called it "A Wow!" *The New York Times* said "It is an ingenious piece of work with a good deal of fun. It growls, whines, squeaks and makes various other sounds that add to its mirthful quality."

Pleased with the success of *Steamboat Willie*, Disney requested that sound now be added to the as yet unreleased *Plane Crazy, Gallopin' Gaucho* and a new Mickey Mouse cartoon *The Barn Dance.* Now he not only had a brand new character to present to cinema audiences, but also three original sound cartoons. Carl Stalling was invited to join the studio and oversee all facets of recording. He later told Mike Barrier: "Perfect synchronization of music and cartoons was a problem, since there were so many quick changes and actions that the music had to match. The thought struck me that if each member of the orchestra had a steady beat in his ear, from a telephone receiver, this would solve the problem."

Although at this time Mickey made only strange noises on screen, he was soon to develop a voice of his own. Walt stepped in and voiced Mickey himself because, as Bob Thomas noted in *The Art of Animation,* "Finally someone said 'Look Walt, you can do the voice exactly the way you want it. Why don't you be Mickey?'" Disney later added, in an interview with the *News of the World* in 1934, "It started from the necessity of saving expenses and doing everything we could ourselves. Naturally, however, it has grown to be a pleasure. And when you hear him talk today you hear

me talk as well. Not that I talk like Mickey all the time!" Disney continued to voice Mickey up until 1946, when Jimmy Macdonald took over – although both Carl Stalling and Clarence Nash, the voice of Donald Duck, had an occasional go at it.

As music began to play a more integral part in each new short, Disney became obsessed with synchronizing music and pictures, even starting to produce a brand new series of cartoons entitled "Silly Symphonies." The use of sound and music effects in films such as *Steamboat Willie* had never been attempted before. For audiences unused to the later sophistication of sound films, the visual and aural delights of the early Mickey films were sheer magic. They were thrilled by Mickey's noisy and daring feats of courage, whether it was rescuing Minnie from all manner of perils or escaping from roaring lions and snapping crocodiles on some distant desert island. As Earl Theisen pointed out in 1937, "Music and sound had become an exact science with Walt Disney. The music and sound effects in his cartoon psychologically tell the film story for the ears as the picture on the screen does for the eyes."

FROM BLACK AND WHITE TO COLOUR

Mickey Mouse appeared in over seventy black and white cartoons up until his colour début in *The Band Concert* (1935). His film career had already spanned six years of variety and entertainment and had contributed to the demise of the one-reel custard-pie comedies, the very films that had influenced Disney so much as a boy.

The early live-action comedies had cost anything up to $40,000 to produce; even the most expensive of the Mickey shorts cost a mere $25,000. But the Mouse with the jet black, saucer-shaped ears was now more popular with audiences than Harold Lloyd, Buster Keaton or The Keystone Kops.

"In some pictures," Disney told *American Cinematographer* in 1932, "he has a touch of Fred Astaire; in others Charlie Chaplin and some of Douglas Fairbanks, but in all of these should be some of the young boy!"

"Mickey Mouse lives in a world in which space, time and the laws of physics are null," *Time* magazine suggested in 1931. "He can reach inside a bull's mouth, pull out his teeth and use them for castanets."

An early model sheet shows the various poses Mickey adopted during his attempt to conduct the orchestra in *The Band Concert* (1935).

Audiences didn't seem to mind Mickey's abuse of his fellow creatures, but, as the cartoons increased in popularity, Disney gradually toned down the cruelty. This was a major step forward in a medium where violence was not so commonplace. "We might note'" Christopher Finch pointed out in *The Art of Walt Disney*, "that the callous attitude displayed by Mickey and Minnie towards other animals made it quite clear that, although not human, these were not ordinary mice. They were creatures invested with special powers. They wore clothing and parodied the habits of men and women. In this respect they belonged to a tradition that goes back to Aesop and Aristophanes."

Mickey was, in fact, at his best when spoofing his human counterparts. For example, Al Jolson's *The Jazz Singer* became *The Jazz Fool* (1929), and in *The Pet Store* (1933) Mickey was rescuing Minnie from the amorous attentions of a large ape inspired by a film magazine showing King Kong on top of the Empire State Building with Fay Wray.

In his early films, Mickey relied heavily on "sight gags" for the majority of his laughs. In *The Karnival Kid* (1929) his fans discovered that he possessed the ability to remove the top portion of his head and ears like a hat. These gags were derived from the heyday of Oswald the Lucky Rabbit.

By the early 1930s Hollywood had discovered colour photography, and Disney was determined to capitalize on it. Half-way through production of a Silly Symphony entitled *Flowers and Trees* (1932), he signed a contract to use Technicolor's unique three-colour process, on the strict understanding that *his* would be the only cartoon film studio licensed to use the technique for a two-year period. *Flowers and Trees*, subsequently re-shot in colour, proved to be a tremendous hit. From then on all the Silly Symphonies were made in colour, but Disney decided that, initially, Mickey Mouse would have to remain in black and white because of the costs involved.

But finances improved, and, in 1935, Mickey starred in *The Band Concert*, his first colour film. Mickey played a band leader who was not only plagued by a swirling tornado while trying to conduct the "William Tell" Overture but who also fell foul

of Donald Duck's performance of "Turkey in the Straw" on a penny whistle. Even though two black and white shorts, *Mickey's Service Station* and *Mickey's Kangaroo*, were released after *The Band Concert*, the gamble of producing Mickey Mouse in

colour had paid off. Some of the earlier black and white stories were re-made. *Orphans' Benefit*, in which Mickey teamed up with Donald for the first time, was originally released in 1934 and re-made in 1941; *The Birthday Party* (1931) became *Mickey's Birthday Party* in 1942.

With the introduction of Technicolor, the animation in Disney films became far superior to that of other studios. Artists and intellectuals began to admire the Disney style. Gilbert Seldes wrote of *The Band Concert* in September 1937, "I know of no other Mickey Mouse in which all the elements are so miraculously blended. It has comedy of detail – such as the sleeve of Mickey's oversized uniform continually slipping down to conceal his baton . . . It has comedy of character in the stern artistic devotion of Mickey contrasted with the unmotivated villainy of Donald; it has

In his first Technicolor adventure, *The Band Concert* (1935), a determined Mickey Mouse led his own orchestra in an amazingly spirited rendition of Rossini's "William Tell" Overture.

Mickey concentrated on his simple sewing chores in *Brave Little Tailor* (1938) before embarking on a "giant sized" adventure.

Above: Mickey performed a number of stunning illusions in *Magician Mickey* (1937), including conjuring up a handful of Donald Ducks. Right: This radiant face appeared on the opening of every Mickey Mouse cartoon.

comedy of action when the tornado twists the entire concert into the air and then reverses itself and brings the players back to the grandstand."

Dilys Powell, writing in *The Saturday Book*, said of the film: "The dovetailing of the two compositions was as perfect as Mickey's discomfiture was spectacular.

This time Donald was the winner. But something in the obstinacy with which he filled in the pauses each time Rossini and Mickey stopped for breath might have warned the onlooker that here was a being doomed to perpetual struggle."

Mickey's colour classics continued. Although his companions starred in a multitude of rival films, shorts such as *Thru the Mirror* (1936), *Magician Mickey, Clock Cleaners, Lonesome Ghosts* (all 1937), *Mickey's Trailer* and *Brave Little Tailor* (both 1938) firmly established Mickey in the mould of a hero. In 1935, Mickey celebrated his seventh birthday. The press coverage this great event garnered certainly re-inforced the public's growing awareness of how important a figure he had become. Cholly Wood in the *Bridgeport Connecticut Herald* (29 September 1935) said of Mickey: "At the age of seven, Mickey Mouse puts to shame all the child prodigies that have ever warmed fond parents' hearts. Mickey Mouse has had more honours showered upon him than many an international or historical hero."

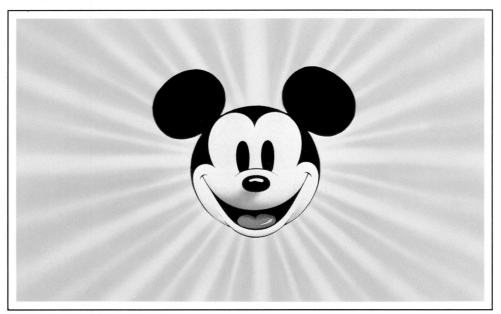

INTERNATIONAL MOVIE-STAR

"There's a certain animile, making everybody smile," ran the lyric of a 1930 popular song by Harry Carlton; "What's this fellow's name? Mickey! Mickey! Tricky Mickey Mouse!"

In that same year, a waxwork figure of Mickey playing the piano, as he had done in his 1929 film *The Opry House*, joined the famous and the infamous at Madame Tussauds in London.

Although only two years old, Mickey was already an established star with a huge international following. More than that, he had become a legend, an authentic creation of 20th-century folk-lore. Mickey Mouse Clubs were formed in many countries, and, by 1932, the American clubs alone had enrolled over one million members.

By the following December, Mickey's popularity was greater even than that of Santa Claus, and he had succeeded in replacing that seasonal gentleman as the Christmas attraction in many of America's department stores. And, in 1935, the Goodyear Rubber Company produced a 50-foot high inflatable Mickey Mouse to lead Macy's Thanksgiving Day Parade in New York.

An astonishing range of Mouse merchandise was now being produced. There were Mickey Mouse toys, games, books and records, and his likeness decorated everything from babies' potties to diamond bracelets and the highly popular Mickey Mouse watch by Ingersoll, of which some 900,000 were sold in just one year.

Comic strips of Mickey's adventures were being syndicated in a dozen countries, and his movies were so popular that, during 1933, it was estimated that there had been over 468 million cinema admissions to see him. And that same year, the *Saturday Evening Post* published a cartoon by Bemelmans showing an American Indian carving a totem pole with traditional birds and beasts, while his papooses called out: "Hey Pop – you forgot Mickey Mouse."

Mickey's fame had succeeded in crossing all cultural and linguistic barriers, and at the peak of his popularity, almost every article written about Mickey Mouse contained anecdotes of his foreign exploits. When fellow film-star Douglas Fairbanks went off on a world tour he, apparently, showed Mickey movies to the head-hunters

Above: In *Mickey's Polo Team* (1936) Mickey, Goofy and the Big Bad Wolf challenged a team of Hollywood celebrities, including Charlie Chaplin and Oliver Hardy. Right: Walt and Roy Disney had plenty to smile about when, in 1932, Walt was given a special Academy Award for creating Mickey Mouse.

of the South Sea Islands (although not, presumably, any of those in which Mickey had to fight off cannibals!). And travellers visiting South Africa reported that the natives were reluctant to accept cakes of soap without Mickey's image on them – just as they had once declined coins that did not carry a portrait of Queen Victoria.

Correspondents wrote that Mickey had a popular following among the Eskimos of Alaska. In both India and Sweden, it was said, cinema-goers would settle for nothing less than seven or eight Mouse films at a time, while, in 1934, Harold Butcher wrote in the *New York Times*, that in the street bazaars of Tokyo the tourists bought Japanese dolls while the Japanese bought models of Mickey. In Yugoslavia, Mickey was suspected of having revolutionary aims; in Russia his films were viewed as a "social satire" on capitalism, and, according to the Director General of the Cinematography Institute of the USSR, Mickey Mouse was "of cosmic value."

Germany, on the other hand, was rather less enthusiastic. In July 1930, the country's film censors banned Mickey's film

The Barnyard Battle, because "the wearing of German military helmets by an army of cats which opposes a militia of mice is offensive to the national dignity."

Mickey remained unabashed, confident in the knowledge that he had the unhesitating support of many world leaders and statesmen. Among those who expressed their affection for Mickey were President Roosevelt, King George and Queen Mary, Benito Mussolini, Mahomet Zahir Khan the Nizam of Hyderabad, William Lyon Mackenzie the Prime Minister of Canada and Field Marshal Jan Christian Smuts. Mickey's younger admirers included the boy King of Siam and Princess Elizabeth, the future Queen of England.

With such world-wide popularity, it is not surprising that, in 1935, the League of Nations should have presented Walt Disney with a special medal in recognition of the fact that Mickey Mouse was "a symbol of universal good will."

A year earlier, Mickey had been given his own entry in the *Encyclopaedia Britannica*, and the hero of the common people found himself being flattered and feted by the intelligentsia. John Betjeman, the poet, and E.M. Forster, the novelist, spoke in praise of Mickey, and the great British cartoonist, David Low, went so far as to describe the Mouse's creator as "the most significant figure in graphic art since Leonardo da Vinci."

In 1934, the British Art Workers Guild elected Walt Disney an Honorary member; and, the following year, an exhibition of Mouse-art was mounted in London's fashionable Leicester Gallery. Other exhibitions followed, on both sides of the Atlantic, and in 1939 a Disney cartoon celluloid was hung in New York's Metropolitan Museum of Art. Writing in the *Woman's Home Companion* in 1934, Alva Johnston commented: "Poor Mickey is in the hands of the dilettantes. After escaping hundreds of other dreadful perils, he is now in the most desperate plight of his career."

However, Mickey had never been the type of guy to be easily taken in, and he refused to let the adulation of the art world go to his head. He carried on making the same kind of movies he had always made and remained as popular with ordinary cinema-goers as ever. Film critic, C.A. Lejeune, called his movies "the most imaginative, witty, and satisfying productions that can be found in the modern cinema;" and the renowned Russian director, Sergei Eisenstein, described Mickey as "America's greatest aesthetic achievement."

Others, however, were not so sure. In 1934 *The New Yorker* cartoonist Alain depicted a group of Manhattan aesthetes in animated discussion, with one remarking: "All you hear is Mickey Mouse, Mickey Mouse, Mickey Mouse! It's as though Chaplin never lived." And in a cartoon by Karl Arnold in the German magazine *Simplicissimus* Mickey was shown stealing the limelight from other popular heroes, including Charlie Chaplin.

There was, however, enormous mutual respect between Chaplin and Disney. Chaplin had been Walt's childhood hero (he had given impersonations of Charlie's little tramp at local theatre amateur nights), and, *Screenland* reported, "Disney blushingly admits that in Mickey he attempts to emulate the wistfulness and the charm of Chaplin." In the same article Disney described Chaplin's movies as "the most humane, as well as the funniest, documents the screen has ever known." He was, therefore, flattered when, in 1931, Chaplin insisted that a Mickey Mouse cartoon should accompany all screenings of his new film, *City Lights*.

The 1935 Thanksgiving Day Parade, organized by the New York store Macy's, was led by a fifty-foot high Mickey Mouse, here shown being inflated.

Two years later, Disney returned the compliment by inviting an animated likeness of Chaplin, as well as a galaxy of other stars, to attend *Mickey's Gala Premiere*. Among those who crowded into a cartoon version of Grauman's Chinese Theater in Hollywood (in what later turned out to be a dream of Mickey's), were Laurel and Hardy, the Marx Brothers, Harold Lloyd, Mae West and Greta Garbo, who (for once

not wanting to be alone) took Mickey in her arms and showered him with kisses.

In an article in *American Classic Screen* (May/June 1978), John Tibbetts commented on this film: "Mickey is the only character who is not a caricature," adding that the Mouse's *real-life* guests "had to first suffer a sea-change into the realm of linear caricature – a brilliant comment on Mickey's dominant position in the industry. They had to meet him on his own terms."

Some of them were to meet Mickey again when, in 1936, Chaplin, Laurel and Hardy and Harpo Marx were invited to take part in a game of polo against *Mickey's Polo Team*, which included Goofy, Donald Duck and the Big Bad Wolf. In turn, Mickey made guest appearances in other people's movies. He had a cameo role in Laurel and Hardy's *Babes in Toyland* (1934), and the same year, in *Hollywood Party*, he was discovered behind Jimmy Durante's sofa and invited to play the piano for Schnozzle's guests. While in *The Princess Comes Across*

(1936), Carole Lombard, as a Swedish noble woman, told interviewers that her favourite film star was "Meeky Moose."

But for all Mickey's popularity with the Hollywood stars – his fans included Mary Pickford and the Barrymores – he was soon putting them all in the shade. According to a report in *Screenland* in 1935, one theatre marquee in Kansas City displayed the billing: "MICKEY MOUSE also Joan Crawford and Clark Gable."

Some people thought that Mickey's popularity was nothing more than a fad, and movie critic Gilbert Seldes likened the Mouse's appeal to that of the kewpie doll and the teddy bear. But, on 18 November 1932, the Academy of Motion Picture Arts and Sciences presented Walt Disney with an Oscar for the creation of Mickey Mouse. It was Hollywood's acknowledgement that Mickey was indeed a star.

Mickey's stardom brought him top billing on cinema marquees, and special stage shows featuring the Mouse were produced.

THE WORLD OF MICKEY MOUSE

COUNTRY MOUSE AND TOWN MOUSE

Mickey was a country mouse, born and bred. *The Adventures of Mickey Mouse,* published in 1931, begins: "This story is about Mickey Mouse who lives in a cozy nest under the floor of the old barn. And it is about his friend Minnie Mouse whose home is safely hidden, soft and warm, somewhere in the chicken house."

It was a romantically rustic setting, immortalized in the song "Minnie's Yoo-Hoo" from *Mickey's Follies* (1929). Written by Walt Disney and Carl Stalling, it became Mickey's earliest hit:

I'm the guy they call little Mickey Mouse,
Got a sweetie down in the chicken house,
Neither fat nor skinny,
She's the horse's whinny,
She's my little Minnie Mouse . . .

Although in later years Mickey became such a respectable, middle-class suburbanite that it was sometimes difficult to remember that he had risen from such humble stock, his rural background was firmly established from the outset. The choice of a barnyard setting for Mickey's earliest adventures was inevitable, reflecting as it did Disney's own most formative years.

Walt Disney was born in the big city of Chicago in 1901, but four years later, his family moved to a smallholding in Marceline, Missouri. Over the next few years, Walt developed a love and a respect for nature that he never lost and that repeatedly manifested itself in his work.

"We can learn a lot from nature in action," he said many years later. "Among other things this: Each creature must earn his right to live and survive by his own efforts, according to his wit and energy." And that was the basis for most of Mickey's early adventures. Unshackled by any great

A country mouse at heart, Mickey went hunting in *R'coon Dawg* (1951).

responsibilities, his life consisted of surviving confrontations with cats and dogs (later semi-humanized as crooks and bullies), protecting his friends and loved ones, earning a living by the honest sweat of his brow and improving the quality of his life by a diversity of recreations. But Mickey also possessed, and demonstrated, that peculiarly human characteristic – ambition.

In *Plane Crazy* (1928), Mickey constructed an aeroplane, said goodbye to his friends and set off to fly round the world. Even though he didn't actually succeed in leaving the farmyard, he had at least established his aspiration to aim high in life.

"Walt's rise from barnyard to city respectability," wrote John Tibbetts, "was rapid and something of a blueprint for American enterprise. Mickey's rise was no less precipitous and no less determined. They both made fun of city slickers at first and distrusted the rascals all their lives . . . but they were nonetheless bent on leaving the farm."

In 1910, Walt Disney's father sold the farm in Missouri and the family moved to the rather more suburban surroundings of Kansas City, where he purchased a delivery route for the *Kansas City Star* newspaper. For Walt, urban life meant acting as an unpaid newspaper boy for his father, working (during school vacations) as a candy-butcher on the railroad and, in his spare time, entering talent competitions – for cash prizes! – at the local opera house.

Mickey, in his turn, soon left the barnyard and, taking the gang with him, headed for a small nearby town: working for the local storekeepers, and having fun – as well as earning a few extra cents – at the carnivals and vaudeville theatres. The move to town gave Mickey a sense of civic responsibility that, eventually, made it difficult for him to kick over the traces and have quite the same uninhibited fun he had enjoyed down on the farm.

True, he got to conduct the town band, but he did so with an earnestness that now showed in all his endeavours – whether, as leader of the local firefighters, he was rescuing Minnie (who had quit her home under the hen-coop for an apartment in town); or, as a detective, he was uncovering the sinister deeds of a bunch of crooks who were stealing the townsfolk's flannel underwear. Even when indulging in Tom Sawyerish exploits – ghost-busting with Donald Duck and Goofy in *Lonesome Ghosts* (1937) – Mickey was much more serious about the business than his chums.

For both Mickey and his creator, life in

Opposite right: Mickey first made a bid to leave the farmyard in *Plane Crazy* (1928). Once in the city, he became a hard-working mouse in the 1937 film, *Clock Cleaners* (above left), and he bought a stylish suburban house, which provided the setting for several films, including (above) *Mickey and the Seal* (1948).

Right: As head of the
Ajax Ghost
Exterminators,
Mickey went
spectre-hunting in
the 1937 film
Lonesome Ghosts,
while in 1939 in *The
Pointer* (below right)
he and Pluto pursued
more conventional
quarry.

the small town eventually led to a move to
the big city. For Disney the city was
Hollywood; for Mickey, at least in his films
and comic-strips, it was the rather more
industrial surroundings – of Chicago,
perhaps.

There Mickey found many new
employment possibilities: in the
construction industry, running a service
station and, later, working for the municipal
authorities, with Donald and Goofy, in
Clock Cleaners (1937). This turned out to
be a hair-raising Harold Lloyd exploit
hundreds of feet up, among the city
skyscrapers.

Being essentially public-spirited
characters, Mickey and the gang showed
boundless enthusiasm for helping their
fellow citizens: they put on shows to raise
money for the local orphanage, repeatedly
came to the aid of harassed mayors and
perplexed police commissioners and, in a
1935 comic strip, took over a newspaper,
The Daily War Drum, and used it to expose
Peg Leg Pete and a gang of racketeers.

Life in the city was not without its
problems for Mickey, and for several years
he seemed to have no fixed abode. In 1932,
according to the comic strips, he was living
at Clarabelle's Boarding House (and acting

as bell-boy and boiler-stoker), but, four
years later, in the film *Moving Day*, he was
sharing a house with Donald Duck – and
getting evicted by the landlord, Pete, for
non-payment of rent.

Then, in the 1938 film *Mickey's Trailer*,
he was living in a caravan with Donald and
Goofy; and although they parked their
mobile home on the city dump, they used an
elaborate folding back drop, decorated with
an idyllic view of mountains and lakes, to
conceal the vista of telegraph poles, railway
sidings and factory chimneys.

Over the next few years, however,
Mickey's increasing fame brought him the
means to buy a permanent home. Together
with Pluto, Mickey moved into a well-

MICKEY AND MINNIE: A FINE ROMANCE

Mickey's relationship with Minnie grew in much the same way as his popularity with cinema audiences. From the beginning Mickey spent a great deal of his time rescuing Minnie in all manner of adventures. Usually it was from the clutches of Peg Leg Pete, the dastardly villain of the resident Disney stock players. But, as E.M. Forster noted, "Mickey's great moments are moments of heroism, and when he carries Minnie out of the harem as a plant-pot or rescues her as she falls in foam, herself its fairest flower, he reaches heights impossible for the entrepreneur." Therefore, Mickey would find his damsel in distress in a variety of locations from Alaska to Arabia to Medieval England.

In *Steamboat Willie* (1928) Mickey rescued Minnie from Pete's threatening advances; in *Brave Little Tailor* (1938), Mickey knew it would be Minnie's fair hand he would win, if he slew the evil giant. Two years later in *The Little Whirlwind* (1941), such was Mickey's affection for her that he was prepared to work hard, sweeping up leaves in the backyard, for a "fair" slice of Minnie's iced cake.

However, in between rescuing Minnie, Mickey found that building up their

Mickey enjoyed his luxurious master bedroom while Pluto acted as valet in *A Gentleman's Gentleman* (1941).

appointed house, with all modern conveniences, in a very select neighbourhood. This provided the setting for such movies as *A Gentleman's Gentleman* (1941) and *Mickey and the Seal* (1948), and was a far cry from his old cosy nest under the floor of his barn.

But despite the acquisition of comfortable means and middle-class respectability, Mickey never really accustomed himself to city life, and in later years, Mickey (like his creator) tried hard to rediscover his roots. And he never needed much excuse to get back to nature – hunting, with Pluto, in *The Pointer* (1939) and *R'coon Dawg* (1951); vacationing in a log cabin – "MICKEY'S HYDOUT" – in *Squatter's Rights* (1946); establishing "Mickey's Wildlife Retreat" in *Primitive Pluto* (1950); or taking a fishing trip in *The Simple Things* (1953).

Mickey's was a classic rags-to-riches story; his transition from country mouse to town mouse was not only a parallel of Disney's own rise to fame, it was also a perfect example of the realization of the great American dream – the boy from the backwoods who makes good.

As Dilys Powell wrote in 1934: "Never was the American manner of life, in which White House is approached by way of log cabin and the actor qualifies first as a soda-jerker or elephant tamer, better exemplified."

Above: The promise of Minnie's hand in marriage helped to boost Mickey's courage in *Brave Little Tailor* (1938). Right: The music sheet cover for "The Wedding of Mister Mickey Mouse" (1935), with words by Edward Pola, shows a beaming Mickey leading Minnie from the church to the happy cheering of Horace Horsecollar and Clarabelle Cow. Far right: A poster for the 1932 film *Mickey's Nightmare* show a hapless Mickey surrounded by numerous little Mickey mice after he dreamed of marrying Minnie.

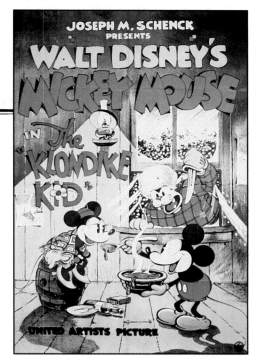

relationship wasn't always easy. In *Mickey's Rival* (1936), Minnie is charmed by a sly-looking rodent called Mortimer, with a flashy sports car. Sometimes Mickey's forgetfulness would get him into trouble as he discovered in *Mickey's Delayed Date* (1947), when he fell asleep in the armchair instead of meeting Minnie at the local dance, and it took all Pluto's ingenuity to save the day.

In the comic strips, Minnie had every reason to be proud of Mickey when he successfully ran his own newspaper in 1935, and although she remained at home, anxiously awaiting news, in *Mickey Joins the Foreign Legion* (1936), she was soon back sharing his adventures in *Mickey Mouse and the Treasure Hunt* (1937).

By now, the question that everybody was asking was, are Mickey and Minnie married? Donald Duck had a girlfriend, but audiences knew that Daisy would never get too romantically involved with such an irascible character; Goofy was a confirmed bachelor, remaining so until the Studio saw fit to turn his lovable hayseed character into an average middle-class man in *Motor Mania* (1950) and *Fathers Are People* (1951); and Pluto courted the dog next door, occasionally finding Butch the bulldog a rival for her affections.

But Mickey and Minnie were the perfect couple, and although a marriage was never shown on screen, it was sometimes suggested that perhaps the happy event had already taken place. In *Mickey's Nightmare*, (1932) for instance, Mickey dreams of wedded bliss in a heart-shaped house, before finding himself father to dozens of little mice. Fortunately, it's only a dream, and, as it occurred early on in Mickey's relationship with Minnie, it may have put him off marriage altogether. Or if they did marry, they must have decided not to tell Walt Disney about it. For in *Overland Monthly* in 1933, Walt said of Mickey: "Sex is not of interest to Mickey: the story of the travelling salesman is of no more interest

than the ladies lingerie department. He is not a little mouse. He only looks like one. He is youth, the Great Unlicked and Uncontaminated." However in the same year, Walt said of his star in *Film Pictorial*: "In private life, Mickey is married to Minnie ... What it really amounts to is that Minnie is, for screen purposes, his leading lady."

Certainly Minnie always shared in Mickey's good fortune. They were a couple who liked the simple life, whether it was a day out in the car or languishing together on some South Sea Isle. But if, because of this, someone asked Disney if Mickey would eventually marry Minnie on screen, the answer was an emphatic "No!" And as he told Louise Morgan in the *News Chronicle* in June 1935 "There's no marriage in the land of make-believe. Mickey and Minnie must live happily ever after."

Above: Mickey was jealous of Mortimer's affection for Minnie in *Mickey's Rival* (1936), but, in 1941, in *The Nifty Nineties* (above right), he found that she had eyes for no one but him.

But this speculation wasn't shared by some of Disney's admirers. E.M. Forster went to great lengths to explain that he felt the Studio kept Mickey and Minnie apart deliberately and too much. "Perhaps even the introduction of Pluto was a mistake," he added. It's interesting to note that in the majority of Pluto cartoons, Mickey seems to prefer living a carefree bachelor life, as witnessed in *Mickey's Parrot* (1938) *Mickey and the Seal* (1948) and *Pluto's Christmas Tree* (1952).

Apart from dreaming about marriage, Mickey found himself romatically involved in the 1945 *Mickey Mouse Annual.* This occurred in an amusing little poem, in which every word began with the letter M: "Merrily Mickey Muttered, 'Marry Me Minnie?' 'My Mascot!' Mused Minnie Meaningly. Minister McMouse Made Modest Minnie Mickey's Missus!" A delightful drawing accompanied the text of the happy couple leaving the church. In 1935 a more ambitious picture, by artist Wilfred Haughton, of Mickey and Minnie getting married adorned the cover of a music sheet entitled *The Wedding of Mister Mickey Mouse* ("By special permission of Walt Disney"), a Novelty Fox-trot with music by Franz Vienna and words by Edward Pola.

Clarabelle the Cow, will jump right over the
  moon . . .
Then you'll hear Pluto croon the latest tune.
Preacher man will see the knot is properly
  tied.
He'll shake hands with the groom, and kiss
  the bride;
Then off they'll go to find their ginger-bread
  house,
Where they'll be happy as Mister and
  Missus Mickey Mouse.

Although some might say, "I told you so," Mickey still denies it. When he was

asked about marriage in the magazine
Funnyworld, he said, "I . . . well, I really . . .
you see, other people are involved here,
and I'm afraid to say anything for fear that I
might hurt them. It's really something
between Minnie and myself. I hope you
understand!" Yes, Mickey we do, but as
E.M. Forster once remarked. "It seems
likely that they have married one another
since it is unlikely that they have married
anyone else, since there is nobody else for
them to marry."

But what about Minnie? Well she's
independent enough. She was once
described as 'Mercenary, Interesting,
Neat, Nagging, Irritable and Exasperating.'
As varied a list of attributes as you could
hope to find, but of all these "neat" certainly
sums up her appearance: little short skirts,
brightly coloured shoes and not too much
make-up. In the early days, a lot of fun was
made of her underwear, she even used it as
a parachute to safely reach the ground in
Plane Crazy. Like Daisy Duck, Minnie was
always fashion-conscious; but, unlike Daisy,
she had the sweetest of temperaments and
the gentlest of voices. In fact over the
years, Minnie had three voices; those of
Marcellite Garner until 1940, Thelma
Boardman between 1940 and 1942 and Ruth
Clifford thereafter.

In all media, Mickey and Minnie's
relationship has proved to be a long-lasting
one. In a cartoon about a fancy dress party
that adorned the cover of *Life* magazine
some years ago, a wife dressed as an Indian
squaw laughingly tells her Mickey Mouse-
suited husband, "I said I'd go as Minnie
Ha-Ha not Minnie Mouse!" And even
today, when Mickey is hosting a Main
Street parade in Disneyland or Walt Disney
World, Minnie is never far behind.

FRIENDS AND FOES

According to *The Adventures of Mickey
Mouse,* published in 1931: "Mickey has
many friends in the old barn and the
barnyard beside Minnie Mouse. There are
Henry Horse and Carolyn Cow and Patricia
Pig and Donald Duck, Clara Cluck the Hen,
Robert the Rooster, all the little Peep-peep
Chicks and Turkeys and the Geese, too.
But the Hound Dog is hardly a friend, and
Claws, the Cat, is no friend at all." Although
all these characters had the distinction of
being among Mickey's earliest companions,
only one or two of them were destined for
stardom – the rest were never heard
of again.

In *Steamboat Willie* (1928), movie
audiences were introduced not just to
Mickey, but also to lovely Minnie Mouse
and to the mean cat who, later minus one
leg, became Mickey's perpetual nemesis,
Peg Leg Pete. The same year, in *Plane
Crazy,* various farmyard animals were seen
helping, or hindering, Mickey as he built an
aeroplane. Among them were ducks, pigs,
goats, dogs, cows and turkeys, but it was to
be a little while before Mickey's "Gang", as
we now know them, made recognizable
screen appearances.

Mickey's closest friends achieved
prominence in the daily comic strips, which

began in 1930. One of the first upon the scene was Clarabelle Cow, who also occasionally appeared under the name of Carolyn Cow. An inelegant, talkative lady with a cow bell round her neck. Clarabelle had a reputation for being something of a gossip. When Mickey and Minnie first met her, on 2 April 1930, Clarabelle talked to Minnie non-stop for an hour. "Wow!" muttered Mickey, "I bet she was vaccinated with a phonograph needle."

Clarabelle's first screen performance had been in *The Plow Boy* (1929), although it is possible that she had made her acting début a year earlier, playing cows in *Steamboat Willie* and *Plane Crazy*. The outstanding characteristic of those creatures were huge sets of udders; but, a few years later, such indelicacies were banned by the Motion Picture Producers and Distributors. In 1934, *Time* magazine reported that "cows in Mickey Mouse cartoon pictures in future will have small or invisible udders, quite unlike the gargantuan organ whose antics of late have shocked some and convulsed other of Mickey Mouse's patrons."

Modestly attired in a skirt, she became

Clarabelle: Minnie's friend and confidant who, according to some later comic strips, ran a boarding-house where Mickey and other members of the gang were residents. Clarabelle was a spirited lady, musically gifted (she played violin and piccolo), and, despite a certain ungainliness, she gave some lively dance performances.

The day after Mickey and Minnie met up with Clarabelle, they bumped into Horace Horsecollar, an equine gentleman in

Mickey's gang were always a musical lot: here Clara Cluck and Clarabelle Cow embark on a duet in *Mickey's Amateurs* (1937).

a derby hat. He had also made his début, under harness, in *The Plow Boy*. But, as Henry Horse in *The Adventures of Mickey Mouse*, he showed himself to be an adaptable character: walking upon his hind legs and possessing a pair of gloved hands, until Mickey suddenly required transportation, whereupon he traded his gloves for a second set of hooves and assumed a more horse-like posture. In the comics, Horace developed into a trusty companion and elder-brother figure for Mickey as well as becoming Clarabelle's beau. Despite the illogicality of such a liaison, he even got engaged to the lady.

Perhaps because Horace and Clarabelle belonged so completely to the rubbery style of early cartoon characters, their movie careers were disappointingly short, although they did appear in a number of Mickey's early films such as *The Beach Party* (1931), *Camping Out* (1934) and *Mickey's Mellerdrammer* (1933), in which the friends staged a production of *Uncle Tom's Cabin* with Mickey as both Uncle Tom and Topsy, Minnie as Little Eva, Clarabelle as Eliza and Horace as the dastardly Simon Legree. And in *Orphans' Benefit* (1934), they danced (or, rather, *galloped*) an unforgettable adagio with Goofy.

Goofy, who for some years had been known as Dippy Dawg, or Dippy the Goof, had first appeared as a bespectacled, peanut-chomping member of the audience in *Mickey's Revue* (1932). But it didn't take him long to establish himself as a well-intentioned, but disastrously clumsy funnyman.

So triumphantly did Goofy get things wrong, he was eventually chosen to replace Horace as Mickey's companion, and was soon accompanying the Mouse, on many of his film and comic-strip adventures – always

The gang shared many pleasant times together – getting back to nature in *Camping Out* (1934) and joining in celebrations for *Mickey's Birthday Party* (1942).

leaving a trail of devastation in his wake.

Another character to rise to prominence in *Orphans' Benefit* was Clara Cluck the Hen, now *Madame* Clara Cluck, "the Barnyard Nightingale." With an outrageous coloratura voice, supplied by veteran actress Florence Gill, and much heaving of her ample bosom, she clucked her way through the sextet from "Lucia," accompanied at the piano by Mickey.

It was in the same show that Donald Duck bravely attempted to recite nursery rhymes, despite constant heckling from the audience of orphan mice. And in 1936, Donald was cast opposite Clara Cluck in *Mickey's Grand Opera*, for which they performed the quartet from "Rigoletto," in a cacophany of discordant quackings and frenzied cluckings.

Although mentioned in passing in the 1931 book *The Adventures of Mickey Mouse*, Donald didn't make his screen début until 1934, in the Silly Symphony film *The Wise Little Hen*, voiced then, as for the rest of his career, by Clarence Nash. Then in 1935, he provided persistent interruptions to the recital in *The Band Concert*, displaying an early knack for stealing Mickey's thunder and demonstrating those temperamental qualities that made him a star.

Another cameo performer, with Donald in *The Wise Little Hen*, was Peter Pig (sometimes known as Percy). Peter went on to make occasional appearances in Mickey's films and comics, often accompanied by his overweight girlfriend, Patricia Pig. So fat was poor Patricia that when, at *The Whoopee Party* (1932), she got up to dance, she took to the floor with a

chair still wedged on her behind. Despite giving a memorable performance on the tuba in *The Band Concert*, Peter, along with Patricia, was one of the first of Mickey's friends to be retired (although they could still be spotted, from time to time, working as extras in crowd scenes).

A far more successful character was Pluto the pup, who was first seen in *The Chain Gang* (1930), as one of a pair of unnamed bloodhounds who got lost while pursuing escaped convict, Mickey. In the same year, he reappeared as Minnie's dog, Rover, causing havoc at *The Picnic*; but, by 1931, he was established as Mickey's dog and, in *The Moose Hunt,* was answering to the name Pluto.

When Walt Disney created his Mouse he was originally going to call him Mortimer but then changed it to Mickey because the name had "a more friendly sound." However, the name 'Mortimer' lingered on – in comic strips as Mickey's mustachioed Uncle Mortimer and, on film, in the guise of a sharp-dressing, fast-talking rat-faced character who toyed with Minnie's affections in *Mickey's Rival* (1936). Despite almost losing Minnie to Mortimer, Mickey

Although Pluto was no pedigree pooch, Mickey didn't hesitate to enter him for the *Society Dog Show* (1939).

In *The Whalers* (1938), Mickey, Goofy and Donald went in for some big fishing, although they only succeeded in catching small fry.

finally managed to oust the interloper, rescued Minnie from a mad bull and won her love once more.

Although it seems likely that Mickey and Minnie were married, they do not appear to have had any family (except in Mickey's worst nightmares!). Perhaps Mickey was put off children by his experiences with his troublesome twin nephews Morty (short for Mortimer?) and Ferdy, or his other nephews and nieces – Morrie, Monty, Maisie and Marmaduke – who lead him a merry dance in the film *Gulliver Mickey* (1934).

During his long career, Mickey has been pitted against many villains of various species. In the movies it was usually Pete the large unshaven feline (possibly related to Mickey's early adversary Claws the Cat), who was invariably cast as a bandit or a gangster.

In the comic strips Pete first appeared as a dumb but fiendish henchman to the weasly Sylvester Shyster, "a crooked lawyer – the kind of guy who'd stick a knife in your back, then have you arrested for carrying concealed weapons." Other rogues included The Gleam, a hypnotizing jewel-thief; The Rhyming Man, a master spy who only ever spoke in verse; Ecks and Doublex, the mad scientists; Dr. Vultur who sought to rule the world from his magnetic submarine; Dr. Grut and his terrifying Aberzombies; and sundry other crooks and desperados who disguised themselves as the Crow, the Bat and the Blot (later known as the Phantom Blot).

Although some of Mickey's friends and foes were to become household names in their own right, none of them – in the early films and comics at least – could have had any existence without the Mouse. Writing in 1949, Peter Ericsson observed: "Mickey himself was indispensable . . . Not the most interesting or even likeable figure of the lot, he was always the pole of normality round which all else revolved in apparent lunacy," exhibiting "an unrefined enjoyment of obvious and corny fun which was immediately shared by children and adults everywhere."

MAKING MICKEY MOVE

EARLY ANATOMY – CIRCLES AND RUBBER HOSES

Early animated cartoon characters were, by their very nature, simple in design. Drawing methods were crude and, as cel animation was so time consuming, there was a limit to just how much detail could be placed in each drawing. Disney's early cartoon creations bore a striking resemblance to other animated characters around at the time. The necessary guidelines on how to animate successfully had yet to be devised, and so the majority of what was being achieved came about through a great deal of trial and error.

Someone who helped to establish those guidelines was Ub Iwerks, Disney's best animator during the 1920s. Because of his understanding of drawing technique and because he was virtually a one-man production line, it was natural that when Disney had the idea for Mickey Mouse he would give Iwerks the job of animating him. As a result Iwerks played a major role in the visual design of Mickey Mouse.

"I evolved him [Mickey] originally out of circles, they were simple and easy to handle," Disney told the *Minneapolis Star* in August 1933. However, he stressed to the artists involved that Mickey's ears should be "not quite" circles. They were quite unique in that they remained "not quite" circles in profile or full face. This made him immediately identifiable to audiences but impossible to imitate in three dimensional models, as toy companies discovered when merchandising Mickey in the years that followed.

To begin with, Mickey had black dots for eyes, a longish snout and tail, pencil legs and a rather jerky walk. His hands betrayed another animator's trick. From 1928 onwards he was drawn with only three fingers and a thumb. "Leaving the finger off was a great asset artistically and financially," Disney commented. "Artistically five digits are too many for a mouse. His hand would look like a bunch of bananas. Financially, not having an extra finger in each of 45,000 drawings that make up a six and one half minute short has saved the Studio millions."

Mickey's circular design seemed to widen his appeal with audiences and was summed up years later by artist John Hench: "He [Mickey] is made out of a series of circles. He is not a static thing but

very dynamic in the way the circles fall together ... So Mickey had made his way while a contemporary known as Felix the Cat didn't get anywhere. He had points all over him, like a cactus." Animator Marc Davis agrees with this theory. "I feel that the circles come out of the quality of moving on the screen without jiggling, whereas with a straight line, or anything with corners, you get a stroboscopic effect."

Veteran animator Ward Kimball remembered one of the secrets behind Mickey's appearance: "drawing Mickey consistently was to use a circle the size of a silver dollar for the close-up shots, a fifty cent piece for medium close-ups, a quarter for medium shots, a nickel for medium long-shots and a dime for long-shots. The head and fanny sections were made with the same size circle and connected with two lines."

To understand how helpful this simple design was to animators, it's appropriate at this point to outline the basic principles for making an animated film. In later years animation techniques improved, and by the time Donald and Goofy appeared on film, the art of animation had become a highly intricate process, involving the skills of

many talented people from storymen and layout artists to draughtsmen and musicians. In the late 1920s, however, things were very different. First a storyboard, a series of rough diagrams illustrating important steps in the film's story, was drawn up. Then a small team of animators, each assigned to different characters, drew them in sequence on to sheets of paper on a lightbox, a sloping table with a thick sheet of glass over a light source, so that the artists could see the drawing or drawings before last and make slight alterations in the movement of the

Above: An early model sheet for Mickey Mouse shows a variety of poses and illustrates the importance of fluidity in the drawings – the circular design for the head and body and the rubbery texture of his arms and legs. Below: Animator Norman Ferguson studied his own facial expressions as a guide to drawing Mickey and Pluto.

characters. These individual drawings were then traced on to transparent sheets of celluloid (cels) by women in the ink and paint department. When completed, the cels were mounted, again individually, over a static background and photographed one at a time using a stop-frame facility on a motion picture camera. Twenty-four separate pictures make up one second of screen time (for sound film) and when projected normally give the drawings the illusion of movement. To keep up with the demand for cartoon shorts 700 feet of film had to be produced every two weeks. That meant an exceptionally large number of drawings, and it was fortunate for Disney that he had Ub Iwerks to produce his first Mickey Mouse film, *Plane Crazy* (1928).

In his early films Mickey's movements were rather stilted. True, he moved in a manner that far surpassed his rivals, Felix or Oswald, but there was little understanding from the animators involved that animation can do a lot more besides suggesting movement. Mickey's arms and legs resembled rubber hoses and the same applied to all of Mickey's companions. This made movement flexible but unrealistic and limited the animators' potential for exaggerating their actions on screen. But with the development of a new animation technique called "squash and stretch," artists were able to use a greater degree of exaggeration and give their cartoons more fluidity.

In Mickey's case, as animator Fred Moore described in his analysis of the character, "The body could be thought of as having a certain volume, so when it is stretched it should grow thinner or plumper as it is squashed." Moore replaced Mickey's circular body with a pear shape. "Now he could get flow, rhythm and flexibility," observed veteran animators Frank Thomas and Ollie Johnston. Mickey expert Les Clark also welcomed the changes: "Using dimes and quarters for Mickey's head was like moving a cut-out across the screen," he said.

Moore later produced a guide to the

mouse's height for future animators. "Mickey is approximately 3 heads high – so from the bottom of feet to body – it should equal a head." In describing Mickey's character, Moore instructed that he be compared to a young boy. "His poses, not only hold poses, but positions of body while walking, running, talking etc., should contain the young boy feeling." And once during a recording session, Disney betrayed to his artists his own ideas on how tall Mickey was supposed to be by holding out his hand and suggesting the height of a child.

Ward Kimball had great admiration for Fred Moore's analysis of Mickey, claiming that Moore was the first artist to escape from the mould of "rubber hose, round circle" school. However, Moore was always extremely nervous of showing Walt any changes he had made to Mickey. Nevertheless Disney would always notice even the most subtle alterations in Mickey's character and once during a screening of a Mickey Mouse cartoon, he turned to Moore and said "Now that's the way I want Mickey to be drawn from now on."

THE MOUSE EVOLVES

In the newspaper strips, Mickey retained his "rubber hose, round circle" image for some time. However, Floyd Gottfredson, who was responsible for the drawings, disliked Mickey's early appearance: "Personally, I think he was stiff and awkward. But, as the years passed we kept trying to evolve him and streamline him, because that's the way animation was going." During the war, the Studio even dropped Mickey's tail, for economic reasons, and informed Gottfredson to do likewise in the strip.

On screen, changes didn't only concern the fate of Mickey's tail. The legs of Mickey's pants were lowered to create the

illusion of shorter legs and his spindly knee joints were covered up. His head was made larger and his ears moved further back. In the comics and on early film posters, Mickey sometimes had pie-slice eyes. These were noticeable in the cartoons only on facial close-ups, but in 1938 his eyes acquired pupils when animator Ward Kimball drew "a new look" Mickey for the cover of a programme for a party celebrating the release of *Snow White and the Seven Dwarfs*. Illustrator Maurice Sendak liked some of these changes, affectionately recalling "the great rounded head extended still further by those black

After being inked by hand, the individual cels are passed on to the next stage in the art of animation. Here Betty Bassett paints the reverse side of a cel from a Mickey Mouse short. On the shelves in front of her are pots of different coloured paints.

Great realism was given to Mickey's appearance in the 1940s; here he sports his new three-dimensional ears in (above) *Canine Caddy* and (opposite above) *The Little Whirlwind* (both 1941).

saucer ears, the black trunk fitting snugly into ballooning red shorts, the tiny legs stuffed into delicious doughy yellow shoes."

During the early 1940s, Mickey's ears were drawn in perspective, that is, they didn't remain circular in all movements of the head. This gave them a three dimensional appearance, and in *The Little Whirlwind* (1941) and *Mickey's Birthday Party* (1942) he even pulled his ears down below his hat brim, something he had never done before – even when wearing a magical hat in his most famous screen role as the Sorcerer's Apprentice in *Fantasia* (1940).

Apart from Mickey himself, his wardrobe changed dramatically over the years. Shoes appeared in his second film *Gallopin' Gaucho* (1928) and, within a few months from the release of *Steamboat Willie*, he began wearing those famous white gloves. Clothes were used sparingly in the early cartoons, again for economic reasons, as they proved complicated to draw. Even during the heyday of Mickey's career he preferred to act out his adventures in little red pants. Occasionally he would dress in something more substantial, such as a bandmaster's coat in *The Band Concert* (1935), even though the sleeves were far too long for him, and a similar problem plagued him when trying to cast spells in *Fantasia*. He almost lost his pants in *Touchdown Mickey* (1932), but recovered his composure for *Mickey's Gala Premiere* (1933) in which he proudly wore a fashionable tail coat. *Hawaiian Holiday* (1937) found him in a grass skirt, and he has worn numerous nightshirts in all manner of

adventures from *Mickey's Nightmare* (1932) to *Mickey's Parrot* (1938).

Alterations in Mickey's sartorial elegance accompanied changes in his personality. From the moment he ceased to be just a little figure made up of black circles, animators began using Fred Moore's analysis of his character as their guide to drawing Mickey. This involved detailing of his head, body and general movement of his arms and legs. Artist Ted Sears also dictated some of Mickey's changes in style. He instructed animators to adhere to Mickey's personality. It was important that Mickey should never appear to be stupid and must behave as realistically as possible.

"Mickey Mouse was the untouchable," according to animator Ward Kimball, "If you made any changes you really had to clear them with 'City Hall' as they say." City Hall being Walt Disney, who controlled the basic guidelines regarding Mickey's character. "In the middle to late 1930s, Mickey

became very pliable," adds Kimball, "This pliability was best demonstrated in *Thru the Mirror* (1936) in which Mickey shrinks to four inches and then grows to hit his head on the ceiling." It was a perfect example of the "squash and stretch" technique, as well as highlighting the sophisticated animation now achieved in the Disney shorts.

It was, however, during Mickey's transitional stage in the 1930s and 1940s, that a great number of veteran Disney animators began looking back with affection on their drawings of the earlier simpler Mickey. Even Walt seemed more devoted to the youthful Mickey, rejecting the more streamlined one. This was also the case with the majority of collectors of Mickey Mouse memorabilia. Collector/artist Mel Birnkrant disliked Mickey's later image, when the studio gave him what he called "cute puffy cheeks, so that his once geometrically pure, round head became an amorphous blob."

But if Walt Disney really did prefer the earlier, less complicated Mickey, so did a number of the Mouse's admirers. Film audiences, Dilys Powell recalled, were "electrified by the apparition of a small acrobatic figure with globular head, protuberant ears and gay inquisitive nose, wearing patched short pants, outsize shoes and the air of a conqueror."

Some critics likened Mickey's early appearance to that of his creator. *Overland Monthly* daringly claimed in 1933 that "Every characteristic of Mickey's from the lift of his eyebrow to his delightful swagger is Walt's own. Mickey is not a mouse, he is Walt Disney."

Disney even began to believe it himself: "The life and ventures of Mickey Mouse have been closely bound up with my own personal and professional life. It is understandable that I should have sentimental attachment for the little personage who played so big a part in the course of Disney Productions and who has been so happily accepted as an amusing friend wherever films are shown around the World." Walt Disney and Mickey Mouse were names that were becoming inextricably woven together, and both were destined to become legends of the cinema world.

In *Thru the Mirror* (1936) Mickey – like Alice in Wonderland – grew so big that he almost filled the house.

MOUSE OF A THOUSAND FACES

AT WORK AND PLAY

Mickey Mouse made his first appearance in 1928, the year *before* the beginning of the great slump. "His emergence," observed Dilys Powell, "co-incided with the years of high living and ballyhoo; and when in *Steamboat Willie*, beaming, he propped open the jaws of a cow and used her teeth for a musical instrument, something in the public mood responded to the confident insolence of his gesture."

Within only a few months, however, came the Wall Street Crash and "honkey-tonk was put in hock." But Mickey quickly adapted to the new mood of society and demonstrated qualities of cheerfulness and endurance in the face of hardships and difficulties.

Mickey was willing to turn his neatly-gloved hand to anything and, uncomplaining, make the best of a bad job. In his very first film, he was to be found working as a deck-hand on a riverboat – steering the craft, loading cargo and peeling potatoes in the galley. Although he didn't seem to have a particularly strong sense of dedication (and showed nothing but contempt for his boss), he did his work in a cheerful, carefree way.

And this was how Mickey approached most of his early occupations: as a teamster in *The Plow Boy*, as a railroad engineer in *Mickey's Choo-Choo,* as a hot-dog vendor in *The Karnival Kid* (all 1929) and as general handyman in *Mickey Cuts Up* (1931), in which he was supposed to tidy Minnie's backyard but – with Pluto's assistance – succeeded in leaving it in a worse mess than ever.

In fact, for some years, employing Mickey could prove a risky, even expensive, business. He always did his best, of course, but things just kept going wrong . . .

For example, Mickey repeatedly tried his hand at being a delivery-man, but never with much success. In the 1932 book, *Mickey Mouse and his Horse Tanglefoot,* he got – and lost – four jobs in as many days: as an ice-man, employee of the Katz Grocery Co., milkman and an agent for a Parcel

Delivery Service. And in *The Delivery Boy* (1931), Mickey was supposed to deliver a wagon-load of musical instruments, but managed, instead, to crash the truck into a barnyard and ended up doing what he enjoyed most – putting on an impromptu musical entertainment for the animals.

Vehicles always presented Mickey with problems – probably because his country upbringing had ill-equipped him for dealing with anything more technical than genuine horse-power. In *Traffic Troubles* (1931), he recklessly drove a taxi to its destruction, ending up on the back of a panic-stricken cow and careering into a hen-house. And, in *Mickey's Steam Roller* (1934), he left the vehicle unattended, and it ran away, coming to halt only when it had completely demolished a hotel.

But not all of Mickey's difficulties at work were of his own making. In *Building a Building* (1933) for example, he was working a steam-shovel when he saw his beloved Minnie (who had been delivering

Left: Mickey demonstrated his light-hearted approach to life in his first screen role as the irrepressible deck-hand in *Steamboat Willie* (1928).

fireman (*The Fire Fighters*, 1930 and *Mickey's Fire Brigade*, 1935), and joined the police force with Donald Duck for *The Dognapper* (1934).

In these and other films Mickey evolved as a leader. Where he had once been a loner, he was now organizing and supervising Donald and Goofy and, in the comic strips, the rest of the gang. Not that it was ever very easy keeping control of such characters, but he was at least notionally in charge of Donald and Goofy's manic activities in *Clock Cleaners* (1937), *The Whalers* (1938) and *Tugboat Mickey* (1940). Sometimes, he even assumed the role of their employer in films like *Mickey's Service Station* (1935) and *Lonesome Ghosts* (1937), in which he ran Ajax Ghost Exterminators.

Having Mickey as supervisor was tantamount to giving Donald and Goofy a licence for unrestricted mayhem, but it also meant that Mickey got very little fun any more. Eventually, the "gang of three"

Hard at work in *Building a Building* (1933), Mickey spotted Minnie's abandoned hat – a clue that she had just been kidnapped by the perennially unpleasant Peg Leg Pete.

packed lunches to the lads on site) being carried off by his boss, the wicked Peg Leg Pete. A terrifying chase across the scaffolding resulted in Minnie being rescued and Pete being floored by a falling girder.

With the passing years, Mickey developed a serious and highly responsible attitude to work; he twice served as a

Ever-courageous, Mickey faced terrible dangers in *Mickey's Fire Brigade* (1935).

became a "gang of two," and Donald and Goofy were let loose on an unsuspecting world without even Mickey's restraining hand.

Although Mickey worked hard, he also played hard, and from his musical larks in *Steamboat Willie* onwards, he never needed much of an excuse to down tools and have a little fun. His recreational pleasures tended to be simple ones – nothing too erudite or sophisticated. He read quite a bit: ghost-stories, thrillers and one or two of the popular classics.

But most of the time, Mickey's chief idea of relaxation was taking time out with his friends for a picnic, a trip to the beach or a camping expedition, or possibly just sloping off with Pluto for a spot of fishing.

When, in later years, finances allowed, Mickey was able to take rather more exotic vacations: to Hawaii, with Minnie, Donald and Goofy, in *Hawaiian Holiday* (1937); and twice, accompanied by Pluto, to Latin America in *Pluto and the Armadillo* (1943) and *Pueblo Pluto* (1949).

Mickey spent most of the rest of his spare time organizing a variety of pastimes and entertainments for the gang.

Occasionally, these were athletic – as in *Barnyard Olympics* (1932) – but mostly they took the form of talent contests and amateur theatricals in films such as *Mickey's Follies* (1929), *The Barnyard Concert* (1930), *The Barnyard Broadcast* (1931), *Mickey's Revue* and *Musical Farmer* (1932), *Mickey's Mellerdrammer* (1933) and *Orphans' Benefit* (1934). At such affairs Mickey was always the producer, director, stage-manager, musical accompanist and master of ceremonies.

Over the years, Mickey's shows increased in sophistication. In *Mickey's Circus* (1936) the gang put on a show to rival Barnum and Bailey, with Mickey as an elegant top-hatted ringmaster.

Analysing Mickey's character, animator Ted Sears wrote: "Mickey is at his best when he sets out to do some particular thing and continues with deadly determination in spite of the fact that one annoyance after another, or some serious menace, tries to impede his progress." Whether at work or at play, whether working on a steamboat or attempting to produce grand opera, that was the hallmark of Mickey's greatness.

Opposite: Mickey encountered a shiver of spooks in *Lonesome Ghosts* (1937) and played ring-master in *Mickey's Circus* (1936).

HERO AND ADVENTURER

When not at work or play, Mickey spent as much time as possible involving himself in all kinds of adventures, most of which resolved themselves with the Mouse triumphant. He was often crowned hero in Minnie's eyes, for he came to her rescue on countless occasions. From the moment they met in *Steamboat Willie,* he constantly found himself in perilous situations in order to save her.

Minnie was always a fair prize for a villainous kidnap attempt. In *The Gorilla Mystery* (1930), a giant hairy escapee from the zoo was so enchanted by Minnie's singing that it broke into her house and terrorized her. It then had the audacity to blow raspberries down the telephone at an anxious Mickey, who rushed to her aid and eventually succeeded in tying up the attacker.

Even worse than a gorilla, to a rare flower of innocence like Minnie, was the evil Peg Leg Pete, who was constantly turning up in a variety of disguises. In *The*

Cactus Kid (1930) – the first western-type adventure for Mickey – Pete, masquerading under the name Peg Leg Pedro, stole Señorita Minnie from under Mickey's nose. Our hero set off in hot pursuit on his faithful steed Pinto and again saved Minnie. As for Peg Leg Pedro, he fell off a cliff and landed painfully on a cactus. Relieved at being rescued, Minnie called after the villain: "Adios, señor, good-bye."

In *The Klondike Kid* (1932), Pete, now alias Pierre, once again kidnapped Minnie. After a daring chase across the frozen wastes, Mickey caught up with Pierre and retrieved his lady-love. And the villain found himself imprisoned when he once again fell off a cliff, this time trapped in a runaway log cabin.

Two years later, in *Shanghaied,* Mickey had to rescue Minnie from a piratical Pete and a gang of fearsome cut-throats. The same villains turned up in the comic-strip adventure *Mickey and the Pirates* (1934), when, in order to deceive Pete into thinking Minnie is willing to marry him, Mickey has to pretend to team up with Pete. There was no end to Pete's villainy: in *Two-Gun*

Below: Having kidnapped Minnie in *The Klondike Kid* (1932), Peg Leg Pete set off across the frozen wastes to escape Mickey's rescue attempts. Right: Thinking that Pluto was following him in *The Pointer* (1939), Mickey got quite a shock when he discovered the truth on one of their numerous hunting expeditions together.

Mickey (1934) he held up Minnie and stole her savings, and in *The Dognapper* (1934) he even stooped so low as to steal Minnie's pet Pekinese, although policemen Mickey and Donald tracked him down to a deserted saw-mill and freed the Peke.

A fearless hero, Mickey never let any danger prevent him doing his duty. *The Fire Fighters* (1930) saw him saving Minnie from a burning building by parachuting them both safely to the ground on a pair of giant trousers. According to the book *Mickey*

Mouse Movie Stories (1931), he later told Minnie:

> Crackling flames and burning house,
> Hold no fright for Mickey Mouse!
> The hotter the fire, the thicker the smoke
> The better he likes it – sezze, "it's a joke!"

In *Pioneer Days* (1930), he and Minnie tried to "go west" until some American Indians caught up with them. Mickey not only saved the day, but Minnie as well. In *Mickey's Rival* (1936), Minnie fell for the flattery of Mortimer Mouse. But the smooth-talking rodent proved too cowardly to rescue Minnie from a bull and it was up to Mickey, once again, to prove that he was worthy of Minnie's affections.

But Mickey didn't perform heroic feats only for Miss Mouse. He could often be found in the thick of battle rescuing his other friends. In *The Mad Doctor* (1933), he saved Pluto from the evil clutches of a maniacal scientist who wanted to use him for various sinister experiments, while in *Mickey's Fire Brigade* (1935), it was Clarabelle Cow (making a rare appearance in a colour cartoon) whom Mickey had to save from a burning house, with the aid of Donald and Goofy. And Donald and Goofy were themselves rescued by Mickey from the gaping jaws of an ocean behemoth in *The Whalers* (1938).

Above and left: There were chilling goings-on in 1933 when Mickey visited *The Mad Doctor*.

IN STRANGE LANDS AND OTHER WORLDS

Considering his size, Mickey has always been an extremely well-travelled mouse. In what was only his second movie, *Gallopin' Gaucho* (1928), he was off in search of adventure. Inspired by Douglas Fairbanks' performance in *The Gaucho* (1927), Mickey donned a serape, leapt on to an ostrich and headed south of the border. There, at the Cantino Argentino, he danced a tango with a sultry Latin beauty, played by Minnie, before duelling for her honour with the villainous Pete.

By 1929, Mickey had become even more adventurous and was seen jiving with a variety of African animals in *Jungle Rhythm*. He returned to Africa – or to a tropical island somewhere off its coast – when, on 13 January 1930, the first of his daily comic strips appeared. For the next two months, Mickey played a castaway, fighting off wild animals and cannibals in a series of dangerous exploits that were to inspire his 1931 film *The Castaway*.

The comic strip *Mickey Mouse and the Seven Ghosts* (1936) saw Mickey dealing successfully with a bunch of phoney supernatural visitors, while in the film, *Lonesome Ghosts* (1937), he fell foul of a group of "high spirited" spooks in an old mansion. But, together with Donald and Goofy, he succeeded in scaring them away forever. In *The Steeple Chase* (1933), when Mickey's horse drank too much liquor before the start, he enlisted the help of his stable hands, dressed them up in a pantomime horse and won the race.

Mickey has faced all manner of dangers on his numerous hunting expeditions. In *The Duck Hunt* (1932), Mickey and Pluto were attacked by some angry ducks and deposited on a washing line, while *Moose Hunters* (1937) found Mickey, Donald and Goofy being chased by a pair of angry moose. In *The Pointer* (1939), when out hunting quail with Pluto, Mickey encountered a ferocious bear.

But whether hero, adventurer or both, Mickey always comes out on top. As the *Bridgeport Connecticut Herald* commented in 1935: "In whatever field he enters, Mickey Mouse is tried, true and efficient. He has never yet had to serve an apprenticeship."

In *Thru the Mirror* (1936), a dreaming Mickey found himself, like Lewis Carroll's famous storybook heroine, in a strange looking-glass world.

Mickey was not the only person in Hollywood to be fascinated by Africa. When, in 1931, MGM made *Trader Horn*, the cast and crew went to Africa for location filming. This was the first such expedition to go out from Hollywood, and it received a great deal of publicity. Less well publicized, however, was the visit made a year later by Mickey and Pluto to film *Trader Mickey*.

Captured by cannibals and put into a cook-pot, the intrepid explorers only just escaped becoming "Dish of the Day." Fortunately, the cannibals discovered a set of musical instruments in Mickey's boat, and released the captives so that they could join in an impromptu jungle jam-session.

Mickey had more problems with cannibals in *Mickey's Man Friday* (1935) when he was once more shipwrecked on a hostile shore. However, in a later comic-strip version of the story, *Mickey Mouse Robinson Crusoe* (1938/39), the whole adventure turned out to have taken place in a Hollywood studio set during the filming of one of his movies.

Nevertheless, the thrill of African exploration never lost its appeal for Mickey, and in a 1949 *Mickey Mouse Annual* he was off to the jungles once more, this time with Horace Horsecollar, in search of the mysterious Goomawallah – although the only creature they succeeded in finding was Donald Duck!

Not that Mickey always went in *search* of adventure, often he just got caught up in one. In *Mickey in Arabia* (1932), for

Mickey's fondness for Medieval history was reflected in a series of costume dramas, including *Ye Olden Days* (1933) and (below) *Brave Little Tailor* (1938).

example, he and Minnie were on holiday when an evil sheik abducted Minnie and carried her off to his harem. Needless to say, Mickey effected a rescue, despite being handicapped by a drunken camel.

In *Alpine Climbers* (1936), Mickey went on a disastrous climbing holiday to Switzerland with Donald and Pluto; while sometime during the 1930s, according to a book entitled *Mickey Mouse on Tour*, they all flew to Britain and visited Loch Ness, the Blackpool Illuminations, Windsor Castle and the Tower of London:

> On to the Tower of London tall,
> Where stern Beefeaters guard the Wall.
> As round the Tower by guides they're led
> "They chopped off *heads* here!" Mickey said.

Mickey had long been interested in historical English drama, and as early as 1933 had made *Ye Olden Days*, in which he played a Medieval minstrel who freed an imprisoned Minnie from an apparently unscalable tower and then jousted with Prince Dippy for the lady's hand. In the 1936 comic strip *Mickey Mouse's Adventures With Robin Hood* Mickey joined the Merrie Men of Sherwood and rescued

another damsel in distress, this time one of Minnie's ancestors, Maid Minerva Rhodent.

His errantry continued in the book *Mickey Mouse Bedtime Stories* (1937), which contained a fairy story about Mickey Stoutheart and his adventures in a fantasy realm populated by elves, dragons, monsters and a fearsome pig-faced giant.

Mickey had first encountered a giant in the 1933 film *Giantland* in which he told his nephews the story of Jack and the Beanstalk with himself in the role of Jack. Then in *Brave Little Tailor* (1938) he played the gentle tailor who told everyone that he had "killed seven with one blow" (referring to house-flies) only to be mistaken for a giant-killer.

These early movie successes inspired the "Mickey and the Beanstalk" sequence in Walt Disney's 1947 feature film *Fun and Fancy Free,* in which, aided and abetted by Donald and Goofy, Mickey took on a homicidal oaf called Willie the Giant.

In *Gulliver Mickey* (1934), it was Mickey who became the giant when – shipwrecked yet again! – he found himself in the land of the Lilliputians. Although loosely based on Jonathan Swift's *Gulliver's Travels,* the book version of the film was entitled *Mickey in Pigmyland,* with Lilliput changed to Pigmalia. Another literary classic about a non-existent world, Lewis Carroll's *Through the Looking-Glass,* was

the inspiration for *Thru the Mirror* (1936), in which Mickey dozed off while reading about Alice's curious adventures and dreamt that he was in a Looking-glass world with an argumentative telephone and a pack of dancing playing-cards, which appeared to have been choreographed by Busby Berkeley.

The popular culture of America provided Mickey with a variety of unusual places in which to make films: Hollywood's "old dark house" movies inspired the weird castles and haunted mansions in such pictures as *The Mad Doctor* (1933) and *Lonesome Ghosts* (1937), while westerns and the novels of Francis Bret Harte suggested scenarios for several films in which Mickey travelled back to the days of the Old West.

In one of his last films, *Mickey Down Under* (1948), he and Pluto visited Australia and had problems with an uncontrollable boomerang and an aggressive ostrich. However, by far the most outlandish locations were to be found in Mickey's comic-strip adventures. In 1936, he joined the Foreign Legion and was tramping

Mickey came eyeball-to-eyeball with an obstreperous ostrich in the 1948 film *Mickey Down Under.*

across the burning desert sands. But that was nothing compared with what he was up to the following year when he visited Sky Island, a curious land supported by atomic power, where the strange Dr. Einmug had his secret laboratory.

Also in 1937, Mickey was having a Ruritanian adventure, impersonating His Royal Highness the Monarch of Medioka and outwitting the wicked Duke Varlett, and in 1941, accompanied by Goofy and paleontologist, Professor Dustibones, he found himself in a lost world inhabited by cavemen and dinosaurs. Three years later, Mickey was journeying forward in time to the World of Tomorrow, where the evil Pete ruled a space-age empire with the aid of a race of robots called Mekka Men.

During the late 1940s and early 1950s, Mickey was teamed with an odd little creature called Eega Beeva, who possessed strange magical powers and a sort of dog called Pflip. A typical story of the period, *The Lost Treasure of Moook* (1950) had Mickey and Eega following a trail of clues through Ireland, England, France, Egypt, Turkey and behind the Iron Curtain. There they were captured by Commissar Peg Leg Pete and carried off to Tibet, where they found Moook and discovered that he was a genie. The story ended with Mickey and Eega taking Moook back with them to the USA and presenting him to the Pentagon as a top secret weapon.

It had taken Mickey a little over twenty years to progress from a carefree globe-trotting adventurer to an important international diplomat.

As maestro, Mickey was totally exhausted by his attempts to finish – against over-whelming odds – a concert in *Symphony Hour* (1942).

SONG-AND-DANCE MOUSE

Ever since audiences thrilled to the tuneful sounds Mickey made in his first screen appearance, he has remained very much a musical mouse. In the early days Mickey was called upon to play a multitude of instruments – pianos, guitars, violins – and, as he showed to startled cinemagoers in *Steamboat Willie,* he could even create highly entertaining music from a number of animals. This was, however, a performance bordering more on cacophony than musical ability. Minnie was there to help out of course. It was she who cranked the goat's tail and produced a raucous rendition of "Turkey in the Straw" while Mickey used a cat's tail as a violin string.

In *The Opry House* (1929), Mickey became the operator of a small town show. Although his concert peformance got out of control, his piano and stool swung in time to the music, one of the first examples of Disney's anthropomorphism of inanimate objects. In *Mickey's Follies* (1929), he sang and danced on top of the piano and in *The*

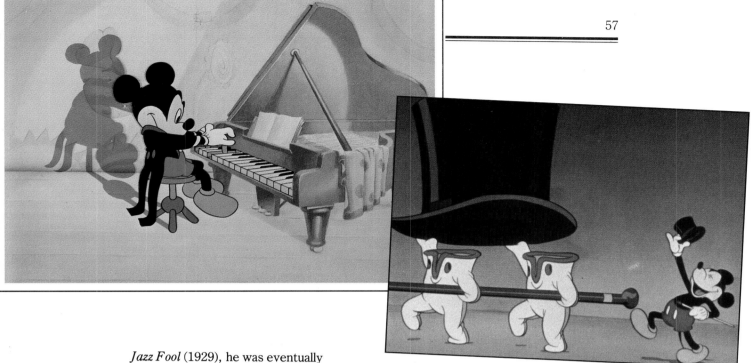

Jazz Fool (1929), he was eventually menaced by the keyboard. In fact, he occasionally fell victim to the instruments he played, particularly crazy pianos.

But, undaunted, Mickey continued a career as a highly talented pianist performing for some extraordinary audiences. In *The Haunted House* (1929) Mickey played for a mansion full of dancing skeletons, and in *The Castaway* (1931), for a bunch of friendly seals who showed great appreciation of the way Mickey tickled the ivories.

In *The Delivery Boy* (1931) it was Minnie who played the piano, while Mickey joined in on the cornet. When the piano was destroyed by an explosion, Mickey and Minnie continued playing on the ribcage of an old mule which, they both agreed, sounded a lot better.

Mickey excelled in playing unlikely instruments and in the 1932 film *The Whoopee Party* made music on a variety of household objects. While Minnie played a version of "Sweet Rosie O'Grady" on the piano, Mickey tapped milk bottles, released mousetraps and flicked a window blind in a

crazy performance of "Running Wild." When the police arrived they too became trapped by the musical frenzy, and the furniture that wasn't already dancing, fell apart around them, as they joined in the fun.

As a saloon pianist in *The Klondike Kid* (1932), Mickey played the piano for money and in *Orphans' Benefit* (1934), Mickey accompanied Clara Cluck's singing, at the piano, even though his fingers became entangled when he tried playing too many fancy notes.

The Band Concert (1935), gave Mickey the opportunity to become a conductor. No longer could a piano get the better of him or even a tornado. He managed to keep the entire band together until the final strains of the "William Tell" Overture had faded away. Only Donald Duck triumphed over the exhausted figure of the conductor. But audiences quickly forgave Mickey for that defeat. As they were soon to discover, very few people get the better of Donald, except Donald himself. In *Symphony Hour* (1942), Mickey got the opportunity to conduct a full

Above right: When not playing a musical instrument, Mickey showed his expertise as a dancer when he accompanied a pair of white gloves, a top hat and a cane in the surreal world of *Thru the Mirror* (1936).

orchestra for a radio broadcast sponsored by Mr. Macaroni, alias Peg Leg Pete. When the instruments were crushed in an elevator shaft by mistake, Mickey had to threaten his friends into finishing the piece. Fortunately, however, Macaroni was delighted with the unusual music made on the broken instruments, and Mickey was once more the hero.

Mickey took up the banjo in the 1945 *Mickey Mouse Annual*, entertaining Minnie as a street musician: "Monday Morning, Mickey Made Modern Minstrel Music. Mickey's Melodies Made Marvellous Money, Making Mickey Merry."

As a performer, of course, Mickey had a wonderful back-up team at the Disney Studio. As Bob Thomas pointed out: "Music so dominated the early sound cartoons that the animator and musician worked in the same office. This spawning ground contained a piano as well as desk and was called the music room. The name stuck for many years after the two basic creators were separated."

Mickey's music was described as having a syncopated beat that was an important addition to the jazz age. "Mickey Mouse music" as it became known, combined percussion and sound effects. As Bob Thomas added, "It stemmed from circus bands and can-can in which the effects corresponded closely to what was happening on the stage or in the ring."

Mickey has also excelled himself as a dancer. In *Mickey Steps Out* (1931), he danced all the way to Minnie's, but the combination of a failed conjuring trick and Pluto's attempts to catch a cat, brought the evening to a swift close. In *Thru the Mirror* (1936), he showed a dancing ability that would make even Fred Astaire envious, performing his tap dancing routines with all manner of everyday objects from matchsticks to a set of playing cards.

When on two occasions the gang

But Mickey's talents aren't limited to those of a song-and-dance mouse. He is also an experienced stage artiste, having performed magical tricks in *Magician Mickey*, in which he got his own back on a noisy member of the audience – Donald Duck; and as a master of ceremonies in films such as *Mickey's Revue* (1932) and *Mickey's Amateurs* (1937). For Mickey there's no business he enjoys more than show business.

As a street entertainer Mickey once sold Pluto to raise money for a poor family at Christmas. Here, performing for passers-by, he is seen on a poster for the 1932 film *Mickey's Good Deed.*

celebrated his birthday, Mickey demonstrated everything from a fox-trot to a hoe-down. When he was given the opportunity of playing the xylophone, it retaliated – unlike the cow in *Steamboat Willie* – and Mickey found himself being hurled around the room by a musical bucking bronco. These rare moments of choreographed brilliance were captured in a 1931 publication called *Mickey Mouse Movie Stories*:

> And then the old xylophone started to
>   prance,
> So Mickey astride of him jumped,
> He capered around with hope, skip and
>   dance,
> And bounded, and pounded and bumped.

Joseph M. Schenck presents WALT DISNEY'S MICKEY MOUSE in "MICKEY'S GOOD DEED" UNITED ARTISTS PICTURE

MICKEY'S WAR AND AFTER

MICKEY'S GREATEST PERFORMANCE

In 1937 Mickey was a star with problems. There was a strong feeling among some of the Disney animators that the Mouse's career was about to enter a decline that might well prove terminal.

Mickey's phenomenal popularity had peaked in 1935, with his first cartoon in colour, *The Band Concert*, which had also introduced the character who, eventually, rivalled Mickey's public appeal – Donald Duck. While continuing to give fine film performances in movies like *Mickey's Garden* (1935) and *Thru the Mirror* (1936), Mickey found himself increasingly upstaged by Donald, Goofy and even his dog, Pluto.

There were a number of aspects to Mickey's character that had brought his career to crisis-point. To start with there was his voice: Disney's excitable falsetto squeak was perfectly acceptable in films in which Mickey concentrated on singing, dancing and slapstick pantomine, but it grew wearisome whenever Mickey had to make extensive use of dialogue.

There were also problems arising from Mickey's established screen personality. By temperament, he was a good-hearted, simple fellow who, as his popularity increased, had become less and less able to indulge in any behaviour that might be construed as naughty or irresponsible. Goofy was allowed to fool around; Donald

could fly off the handle; but Mickey was the good scout who always played things straight.

Then there was the question of Mickey's size. Pluto was a fully grown dog; Donald was the size of a large duck; Horace and Clarabelle were proportionally larger; and Goofy was really a man with rather doggy features. Mickey, however, was an enormous mouse, totally out of scale with everything around him. As one animator put it: "what can you do with a four foot mouse?"

For purely sentimental reasons, however, Disney was reluctant to let Mickey fade into obscurity. The Mouse was a character, born out of adversity, to whom Disney, literally, owed everything he had. In consequence, he was always looking for an opportunity to further Mickey's career. In 1937, while listening to music for possible Silly Symphony projects, Disney chanced upon what seemed an ideal vehicle for Mickey Mouse – Paul Dukas's fantasy scherzo *L'Apprenti-sorcier* ("The Sorcerer's Apprentice").

The music told of an apprentice magician who tried out one of his master's spells and brings a broomstick to life to do his chores for him. The would-be sorcerer sets the broom to work fetching and carrying pails of water, but discovers – too late – that he doesn't know how to *stop* the spell. Seizing an axe, he chops up the broom, only to find that every splinter of wood becomes itself a new bucket-carrying broom. Eventually, when the castle is half under water, the Sorcerer returns and halts the magic.

There were Studio discussions about the idea of making a Silly Symphony based on Paul Dukas's music, but while there was general agreement that it was a good subject, there emerged at least one other contender for the title-role. The Studio's first feature-length animated film, *Snow White and the Seven Dwarfs*, was nearing completion and it was suggested that the

most engaging of the dwarfs, Dopey, should be given the part of the young sorcerer. Walt Disney, however, remained determined that the star of the film would be his old friend Mickey Mouse.

In May 1937, Disney began negotiations to obtain the rights to Dukas's music, and by July these were secured. It was at this point that an important figure entered Mickey's life. One evening, early in 1937, Walt Disney was dining alone at Chasen's restaurant in Beverly Hills when he noticed another solitary diner at a nearby table – it was Leopold Stokowski.

As idiosyncratic conductor of the Philadelphia Orchestra, Stokowski had recently found worldwide fame through his appearance in two movies: *The Big Broadcast of 1937* and *One Hundred Men and a Girl.* Disney invited Stokowski to join him, and the two men took to each other immediately. During a three-hour conversation, Disney told the Maestro that he was planning to film "The Sorcerer's Apprentice," and Stokowski offered to conduct the score.

Both men were excited about the project, with Stokowski writing to Disney to say how thrilled he was about the idea "because you have no more enthusiastic admirer in the world than I am;" and Disney telling his New York representative that "the union of Stokowski and his music, together with the best of our medium, would be the means of a great success."

Preliminary work on the story was soon under way with a Studio memorandum, dated November 1937, referring to the film as "a musical fantasy, offering an opportunity for a new type of entertainment." It was now clear that Mickey was the perfect choice for the role of the Apprentice, since the film was to be made "without dialogue and without sound effects, depending solely on pantomime and descriptive music."

Stokowski, however, had some reservations about working with the Mouse. "What would you think," he asked Disney in a letter in November 1937, "of creating an entirely new personality for this film instead of Mickey? A personality that could represent *you and me* .... You may have strong reasons for wishing Mickey to

A psychedelic film poster used for the 1976 re-release of *Fantasia.* A simulated stereo soundtrack was added to the film in an attempt to approximate to the sound performance Walt Disney had originally envisaged.

be the hero . . . this is merely a suggestion, which . . . discard immediately if it does not interest you."

Disney *did* have strong reasons for using Mickey and Stokowski's suggestion was politely ignored. The music was recorded by Stokowski, with an orchestra of hand-picked musicians, in January 1938, and the film went into production. Disney appointed Perce Pearce as director, although he later left the project to work on *Bambi*, being replaced by James Algar. Among the animators assigned to the film was Les Clark who, 10 years earlier, had animated part of *Steamboat Willie*.

Mickey's appearance in "The Sorcerer's Apprentice" was styled by the Studio's Mouse-expert, Fred Moore, and an important evolutionary change occurred in Mickey's looks. For the first time, on film, he was given eyes with pupils, although movie-goers first noticed this new characteristic in *The Pointer*, which reached the screen before "The Sorcerer's Apprentice."

Disney asked his artists to avoid "slapstick gags in the ordinary sense" and to "work instead towards fantasy and business with an imaginative touch." In one such sequence devised for the film, Mickey falls asleep (while the magic broom is busily at work) and dreams that he is standing on top of a high cliff, above rising seas, controlling the stars and planets of the firmament with the exaggerated gestures of an orchestral conductor.

Although in a later book-of-the-film, the great Sorcerer for whom Mickey works was given the name Yensid ("Disney" spelt backwards), Walt Disney had more in common with the apprentice than with his master. Mickey's lively, boyish character and natural talent for pantomime made him ideally suited to the role of the mischievous apprentice, and his dreams of cosmic greatness were a reflection of his own – and his creator's ambitions.

The film was completed at a cost of $125,000 – three or four times the cost of an average Silly Symphony – and ran at twice the length of any short cartoon. Faced

A first-day cover of one of a set of postage stamps commemorating *Fantasia*, issued in Mongolia in 1983.

with serious problems of distribution and marketing, Disney eventually decided to make "The Sorcerer's Apprentice" one episode in a feature-length film of classical music illustrated with Disney animation.

Musicologist and composer, Deems Taylor, was brought in as adviser and to provide a linking narrative for the completed movie. Stokowski and the Philadelphia Orchestra recorded seven other musical works ranging from Tchaikovsky's "The Nutcracker Suite" to Stravinsky's "The Rite of Spring" and including compositions by Bach, Beethoven and Schubert. The film was provisionally called "The Concert Feature" but later became *Fantasia*.

Fantasia was conceived as a highly innovative film, with Disney exploring the possibility of using a wide-screen and 3-D effects. Although those particular ideas were abandoned, *Fantasia* was recorded using an early form of stereophonic sound which utilized some 90 speakers and was christened "Fantasound."

Fantasia opened, in November 1940, at the Broadway Theater in New York, where – 12 years earlier – when it was known as the Colony, Mickey had made his debut in *Steamboat Willie*.

Bosley Crowther, film critic of *The New York Times*, described the film as "simply terrific – as terrific as anything that has ever happened on the screen." And, while not all the critics agreed with him, everyone was unanimous in hailing Mickey's performance as the greatest in his career. Nevertheless, it took *Fantasia* many years and numerous re-releases to recover its total cost of $2,280,000. Then, in 1982, the film was given a new digitally-recorded sound track and found a new cult following.

At the end of "The Sorcerer's Apprentice" sequence, Mickey (still dressed in his magician's costume) ran up the steps of the conductor's podium to shake hands with Stokowski. Commenting on this famous encounter between the Maestro and the Mousetro, John Tibbetts wrote: "The point had been made . . . The ultimate strength of the 'The Sorcerer's Apprentice' was that Mickey was really in charge, not Stokowski, or even Dukas. Regardless of the rebellion of the splintered brooms, Mickey was the core of the action, the agent of change. While the sorcerer remained a shadowy, forbidding artist-image, Mickey foolish but erstwhile, reflected the real artistic priorities of the world. He had become a kind of artistic custodian, an interlocutor between us and the forbidding sorcerer of art."

"Now, where is that bally cat?"

MICKEY'S FINEST HOUR

At the time of America's entry into the Second World War, on 7 December 1941, Walt Disney was facing many problems: animation costs were rising, and it was becoming increasingly difficult to obtain supplies of essential materials, while the war in Europe had prevented him from recovering any of the money earned there by his movies.

In 1940, Disney had moved to a brand new Studio in Burbank, a few miles north of Los Angeles, and released two very expensive films – *Pinocchio* and *Fantasia* – which, masterpieces though they were, offered no hope of a quick return on his investment. To make matters worse, Disney was committed to a number of other costly and ambitious projects, and in 1941 the Studio was only just beginning to recover from a bitter strike that had resulted in the departure of several talented animators and cost Disney dearly in lost revenue.

The solution to Disney's financial problems came through his decision to diversify into the production of films sponsored or underwritten by government and industry. He had already begun to explore the potential of animation for

purposes other than entertainment when, in 1940, he had made an instructional film for the Lockheed Aircraft Corporation on *Four Methods of Flush Riveting*.

The day after the bombing of Pearl Harbor, Disney was offered a government contract to produce 20 training films and, two years later, such work represented 94 per cent of the Studio's output. He was also commissioned to produce a series of information films for the National Film Board of Canada, designed to encourage the public to buy war bonds.

One of these films, *All Together* (1942), featured a grand parade of Disney celebrities – Donald Duck and his nephews, Goofy, Pluto, Horace, Clarabelle and the Seven Dwarfs – with Mickey in the characteristic role as leader of the band.

He also appeared, *in absentia*, in another information film, *Out of the Frying Pan into the Firing Line* (1942). As Minnie Mouse listened to a voice on the kitchen radio telling her how the conservation of used cooking fat could help provide glycerin for the war effort, Pluto was seen saluting a photograph of Mickey Mouse in uniform.

Long before the Second World War, Mickey was upsetting the Germans. In 1930 they banned his film *The Barnyard Battle* (1929), because, as can be seen from this contemporary postcard, he went to war with a cat wearing German military uniform.

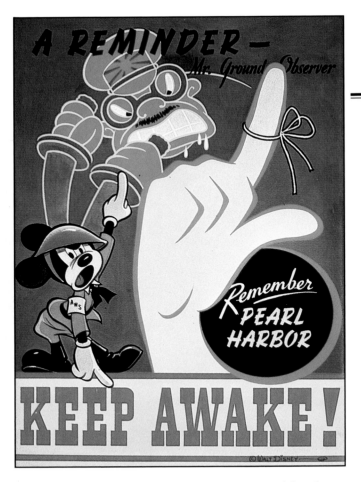

A REMINDER —
Mr. Ground Observer

Remember
PEARL
HARBOR

KEEP AWAKE!

Although it may seem surprising that such an essentially peace-loving character as Mickey should have gone to war, his enlistment was, in fact, the inevitable climax of a long-standing confrontation with Nazism. As early as 1931, a Nazi newspaper had condemned Mickey as "the most miserable ideal ever revealed." German children who sported Mickey Mouse badges were told that "the dirty and filth-covered vermin, the greatest bacteria-carrier in the animal kingdom, cannot be the ideal type of animal . . . Down with Mickey Mouse! Wear the Swastika cross!"

Adolf Hitler himself repeatedly denounced Mickey, and in 1937 he tried to ban Mickey completely from the cinemas of Germany, but so great was the public outcry that the ban eventually had to be lifted.

Unlike Donald Duck and Goofy, Mickey never made any war films, but there is no doubting the fact that he "did his bit" just the same. He was, for example, featured on numerous wartime information posters, and Mickey's comic-strip adventures also showed him working for the war effort. In *Mickey Mouse and the Black Crow Mystery*, which began serialization in August 1942, Mickey and Goofy were working on a farm in order to unmask a saboteur disguising himself as a black crow, and two years later, in *Mickey Mouse and the War Orphans*, Mickey gave a home to three little waifs who turned out to be royal refugees wanted by the Nazis.

Although Mickey's comic strips were popular in Italy, and Mussolini and his family declared fans of the Mouse, the anti-Axis tone of his adventures caused Hitler to insist that Mussolini ban Mickey from Italian newspapers. It has been suggested that this censorship was so unpopular it contributed to the first youth rebellion against Mussolini.

In 1943, Mickey was really in the thick of things with a story entitled *Mickey Mouse on a Secret Mission*, in which he acted as test-pilot for a newly-developed, self-navigating aeroplane called "The Bat." Having destroyed several German strategic centres, Mickey captured the Nazi chiefs of staff while, at the same time, preventing the secret of "The Bat" from falling into the hands of Peg Leg Pete. In 1944, if the cover of a *Mickey Mouse Annual* is anything to go by, he also served with Britain's Royal Air Force, although other contemporary illustrations show him as an infantry soldier and, with Donald Duck, as a member of the tank corps.

Mickey's efforts were so appreciated by the men of the Allied forces that many units wrote to Walt Disney asking for specially designed insignia featuring the Mouse and his friends. At its own expense the Studio produced some 1200 such insignia for the troops to wear as shoulder-patches or with which to decorate their tanks and planes.

Mickey also appeared in a sailor's beret,

AIRCRAFT WORKER

BUILDING PLANES FOR VICTORY

© WALT DISNEY

The huge popularity of Mickey among the young, inspired the Sun Rubber Company of Ohio to design a Mickey Mouse gas-mask, intended to "lessen the fear of gas-attack for children by taking the conventional gruesome-looking gas-mask and turning it into something fun". Since it eventually became clear that there was little serious threat of gas-attacks on America, the mask never went into production. But in Britain – where everyone, including children, had to carry gas-masks – a similar idea was adopted and what was officially known as the "Small Child Respirator" was popularly nicknamed "the Mickey Mouse gas-mask."

Recalling his childhood in wartime London, writer Bevis Hillier has written: "In a moment of rubbery inhalation I was introduced to Mickey Mouse, I touched him. More than that, I looked out on a world of blitzed buildings and bomb shelters through his eyes. I *was* Mickey, a flesh-and-blood effigy of a celluloid figment."

And while Mickey's likeness was helping children on the home-front, Mickey himself was playing a crucial role in the great struggle for world peace. His finest hour came on D-Day – 6 June 1944 – when the password chosen for the Allied invasion was "Mickey Mouse." If Hitler ever heard about that, it must have given him pause for thought.

Opposite: To encourage the public to do their bit, Mickey and the gang were featured on a series of wartime information posters, while (left) the Studio produced specially designed insignia for the armed forces and war workers.

aiming a catapult from the back of a leaping swordfish, on an insignia designed for one of London's Motor Gun Boats, and, dressed in an army field uniform, a saluting Mickey Mouse provided the emblem for the Junior Victory Army of America.

MICKEY MOUSE ANNUAL

DEAN

FUN AND FROLICS

The Simple Things (right), which was made in 1953, was Mickey's last screen appearance for thirty years.

After a stunning performance as the Sorcerer's Apprentice in *Fantasia* and a rather subtle entry into wartime propaganda, Mickey found himself back making cartoon shorts. One, entitled *Symphony Hour* (1942), gave him the opportunity of imitating the great Leopold Stokowski when Mickey was invited to conduct a performance of the "Light Cavalry" Overture.

From the active, rebellious little character he played in the 1930s, Mickey was by now very much a suburban mouse, although, apart from conducting, he still got himself into the occasional scrape. In *Mickey and the Seal* (1948), for example, he unwittingly brought home a mischievous stowaway from the zoo. Of the eight shorts, Mickey made between 1947 and 1953 only two, *Mickey Down Under* (1948) and *The Simple Things* (1953), were vehicles for his expert comedy.

By the end of the 1940s, audiences

began to wonder whether Disney would give Mickey another comeback. But after *Fantasia*, the Mouse's only other feature film appearance was that of a starving farmer in *Fun and Fancy Free* (1947), starring Edgar Bergen, with his dummies Charlie McCarthy and Mortimer Snerd and the voices of Dinah Shore and Cliff Edwards. *Fun and Fancy Free* comprised two separate stories introduced by Jiminy Cricket and linked by Bergen. The first related the tale of Bongo the Circus Bear, the second told how Mickey, with the aid of Donald and Goofy, rescued the Singing Harp from the evil giant, Willie, and restored Happy Valley to its former splendour. This all took place in Mickey's own version of "Jack and the Beanstalk."

The critics welcomed the film when it was released, Bosley Crowther of *The New York Times*, particularly enjoying the Mickey section. But while Leonard Maltin thought the sequence was "a nice variation on the classic fairy tale, with some particularly bright touches," he also admitted that it was "hardly of feature film calibre, looking more like just what it is: an elongated short subject."

A few years earlier a cartoon entitled *Pluto and the Armadillo* (1943), in which

Mickey and Pluto visit South America, failed to be included in the short feature, *Saludos Amigos,* for which it was probably destined. *Saludos Amigos* resulted from a goodwill tour, sponsored by the American

Government, which the Studio made in 1941.

Even though Mickey didn't get the opportunity to appear in *Saludos Amigos,* it was of little importance as most of the gags with the armadillo centred around Pluto anyway. In fact, Mickey began to take more of a back seat to the canine cavortings of his favourite pet, and during the same period Donald and Goofy, unlike Mickey, appeared in well over a hundred different cartoon shorts.

In the comic strips, however, Mickey still showed his superiority over his companions. When Goofy became quite big headed about success in the story *Hollywood* (1951), Mickey quickly cut him down to size and made him see sense. Even though he wasn't about to let his friends steal all the limelight, his own film career still created difficulties for the Studio. "Mickey's our problem child," Disney said in 1953. "He's so much of an institution that we're limited in what we can do with him . . . Mickey must always be sweet, always lovable. What can you do with such a leading Man?"

Mickey couldn't wait to discover what wonderful surprise awaited him beneath the wrapping paper and ribbon in *Mickey's Birthday Party* (1942).

Even as early as 1949, Mickey or perhaps more accurately, Walt, was being wooed by the wonders of television, but if he had any future plans for the Mouse, he was keeping them secret: "I'm tired of Mickey now," he commented in 1951. "For him it's definitely trap time ... The Mouse and I have been together for about 22 years. That's long enough for any association." This was a time when Disney was excited by the potential of live action films. *Treasure Island* (1950) had just been released to great acclaim, and he was also making plans for his most ambitious project, Disneyland, which was due to open its doors to the public in 1955.

So perhaps Mickey deserved the break. He had, after all, founded an empire and been responsible for a staggering number of films before Donald and Goofy had even started. With short subjects such as *Pluto's Christmas Tree,* Mickey was taking early retirement from the movies. And it certainly was early. He still hadn't reached his twenty-fifth birthday.

But television, something that Hollywood frowned upon during the 1940s and 1950s, wanted Mickey. BBC Television, had, in fact, already screened a number of Mickey shorts before and after

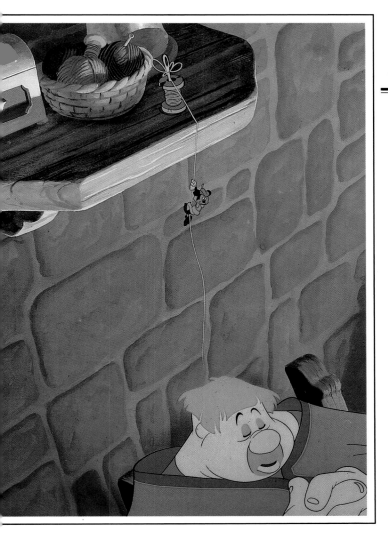

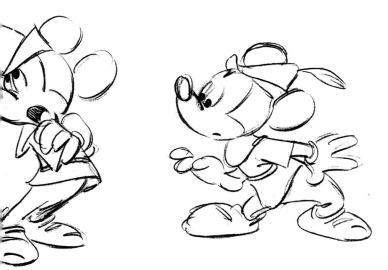

the war. In 1936, television producer Cecil Madden, was given permission by Walt to show black and white Mickey cartoons, and it was *Mickey's Gala Premiere* that was interrupted when BBC Television closed down at the outbreak of the Second World War, and began the first day's transmission when the war was over.

By the 1950s, Disney knew that if American television wanted Mickey, then it had to be on his own terms. "Mickey's been my passport to everything I've wanted to do," Disney told *The New York Times* in 1953. "When I felt I should branch out a little – I wanted to try pure beauty in cartoons. I wanted to try animating great music. I had a lot of ideas – but all the exhibitors wanted was Mickey. Okay I gave them Mickey, but they had to take my Silly used over their heads."

The Mouse made his last film for thirty years, *The Simple Things*, in 1953 before moving to television and then on to Disneyland and Walt Disney World. And as far as a future film career was concerned? Well, as Disney once remarked in an interview regarding Mickey Mouse, "as long as there's a Disney Studio, there'll be Mickey Mouse cartoons. I can't live without them."

Above: In a rare still showing Mickey's eyelids, an unusual visitor popped up out of the bathtub in the 1948 short *Mickey and the Seal*. In the "Mickey and the Beanstalk" sequence from *Fun and Fancy Free* (1947), Mickey traded the family cow for a box of magic beans (opposite). These grew into a beanstalk that transported him – together with Goofy and Donald – to a castle in the clouds, where he encountered Willie the Giant (left).

MOUSEMANIA

MARKETING THE MOUSE

All over America there are specialist stores where Mickey's fans can purchase such vintage items of mouse merchandise as a cast-iron Mickey Mouse money-bank, or a Mickey Mouse radio (decorated with a figure of Mickey playing a double-bass) or a set of Mickey Mouse film-soundtracks on 78 r.p.m. records, or even a 1934 Post Toasties Corn Flakes box with cut-out figures of Mickey, Minnie, Pluto and the gang.

Mouse collectors join clubs, attend conventions and keep a careful check on the kind of prices fetched in auction rooms whenever a Mickey Mouse watch or a wind-up toy goes under the hammer. In fact, so much Mouse merchandise has been produced during the past six decades, that lists have been made, catalogues compiled and several books written on the subject.

Today, character merchandising represents a substantial percentage of The Walt Disney Company's annual income, but its beginnings were modest.

In 1929, Walt Disney was in New York and, he later recalled, "a fellow kept hanging around my hotel waving $300 at me and saying that he wanted to put the Mouse on the paper tablets children use in school. As usual, Roy and I needed money, so I took the $300." Since no one is known to possess one of these writing-pads, it may never have been manufactured – or perhaps it is just the rarest of all Mickey Mouse collectibles.

In the same year, to administer a variety of ancillary activities, Walt and Roy set up Walt Disney Enterprises, a division of the company that eventually handled Disney merchandise worth millions of dollars – something the brothers could never have envisaged in 1929, even in their wildest dreams.

Disney did have some experience of character merchandising: Oswald the Lucky Rabbit had appeared on button badges, the waxed-paper wrapper of milk chocolate Frappe Bars and a child's stencil set. But he was in the film business, not in the toy or confectionary trade, and it took him some while to fully appreciate the benefits that character merchandising could offer, both in terms of valuable licence fees from manufacturers and as a way of increasing public awareness of the Studio's characters. After all, in 1930 Mickey was one of the most popular stars of the movies.

The first Mickey Mouse toy came about somewhat by chance. An enterprising lady called Charlotte Clark, who earned her living by making and selling novelties, decided to capitalize on Mickey's enormous appeal and produce a Mickey Mouse soft toy. Mrs. Clark asked her nephew, Bob

Walt Disney pictured with soft toys made by Charlotte Clark – one of the earliest examples of Mickey Mouse products.

Clampett, who was a keen amateur artist, to design the doll for her, and he made some sketches from "life" at his local cinema. From these drawings, and with Clampett's help, Charlotte Clark produced the first stuffed Mickey Mouse doll.

Mrs. Clark's toy bore such a striking resemblance to the real Mickey Mouse that she was warned'that, as he was a copyrighted character, she should ask Walt Disney's permission before putting the doll into production. However, Walt and Roy were delighted by the toy and rented a house for Charlotte Clark near the Studio (later known as "The Doll House") where she could make more Mickeys. She employed six young women to work with her and the doll's designer, Bob Clampett, helped by stuffing the toys with kapok.

Bob Clampett later became well known as an animator, and was responsible for drawing the first Bugs Bunny cartoon and creating the famous cat and canary characters, Sylvester and Tweetie Pie.

At first, the dolls were given away to friends, business associates and Studio guests, but when Walt was pictured with one of the toys in *Screen Play Secrets*, it created an immediate public demand, and by November 1930, Charlotte Clark was making up to 400 dolls a week, and these were sold for $5 each.

Earlier the same year, Disney had signed a major merchandising contract with the George Borgfeldt Corporation of New York, which, on 27 March, issued its first license to Waldburger, Tanner and Company of St. Gall, Switzerland, for the manufacture of Mickey and Minnie Mouse handkerchiefs.

Three months later, Walt appointed Williams Banks Levy as his merchandising representative in London. Levy, who was a manager in England for Powers Cinephone, soon had several British manufacturers interested and, by September 1930, had organized an impressive line-up of Mickey merchandise, including dress fabrics, fountain pen clips, balloons, tablecloths, egg

By the early 1930s, Mickey Mouse was featured on a wide range of American merchandise. Walt Disney poses among some of the hundreds of dolls, toys, books and games featuring Mickey's likeness.

During his career Mickey has endorsed all manner of products: here he was helping to sell Ritz Crackers, Fig Newtons and other products from the National Biscuit Company in the film commercial *Mickey's Surprise Party* (1939).

cups, toothbrushes, candles and calendars, nursery wallpaper, and a Mickey Mouse "jazzer" – a small felt Mickey, which when attached to the needle-arm of a phonograph, danced about on the revolving record.

October 1930 saw the appearance of the first British Mickey Mouse doll, made by Dean's Rag Book Company; but it had a strange toothy leer, which gave the character an unappealing, sinister appearance. In America, Disney had similar problems with the Mickey Mouse doll designed by Borgfeldt, which, Walt and Roy felt, was a poor representation of their star.

In a letter to Borgfeldt, in October 1930, Roy Disney wrote that they wanted "to be sure that the doll put out is a good one, and a good likeness to our character." But the problems went on, with Walt and Roy complaining that Borgfeldt's dolls either had legs that were too thick, feet that were too small, gloves that were too big or a mouth that was "crooked and not as we like it." Roy told the manufacturer that he was disappointed and that Walt was "positively disgusted," and that the appearance of the Mickey Mouse toy was more important than "the mere royalties involved in the sale of the dolls."

In 1932, Disney decided to resolve the problem by allowing McCall's to publish the pattern for Mrs. Clark's Mickey Mouse doll, so that people could make the toy for themselves. Two years later, Charlotte

Clark went to work as a designer for the Knickerbocker Toy Company of New York City, and quality Mickeys and Minnies – together with Horaces, Clarabelles and Plutos – were finally produced by a reputable manufacturer.

However, Disney continued to be dissatisfied with the quality of much of the other merchandise being sold in Europe and America, and he was looking for a solution to his problems when, in 1932, he received a telephone call from Herman "Kay" Kamen, who had founded the Kansas City advertising agency Kamen-Blair, and who was generally regarded as one of the finest promotional men in America.

Kamen offered Disney his services and was contracted as Disney's representative in matters of character licensing, with the

understanding that he would become their sole agent when the contracts expired with Borgfeldt in America and Levy in Britain. (In fact, Levy maintained his link with Disney, in 1936 launching the *Mickey Mouse Weekly* comic with Odhams Press Ltd.)

In 1932, United Artists produced a 48-page campaign book showing theatre managers how to promote Mickey Mouse films through co-operation with local store-keepers selling Disney merchandise. This book and the seven merchandising catalogues that Kamen produced from 1934 to 1949, were distributed to thousands of exhibitors, manufacturers and traders.

These catalogues show the staggering extent of Mouse merchandising that was available: there was nursery china and cutlery, brush-and-comb sets; buckets and spades; lunch-tins; hot-water bottles and cookie-cutters; neck-ties and hair-ribbons; stationery and painting-sets; rocking-chairs and garden slides; toy drums and pianos; bagatelles, hoop-las and shooting-games; night-lights and modelled soap figures; a Mickey Mouse "movie-jecktor" and a Minnie Mouse car-mascot posed like the Rolls Royce flying lady.

Once Kay Kamen became Disney's sole merchandising representative, in 1933, he adopted stringent measures to deal with previous shortcomings, cancelling all those contracts with manufacturers that failed to comply with Disney's standards.

Kamen's approach proved highly successful: in one of his first deals, he sold a licence to America's National Dairy for 30,000,000 Mickey Mouse ice-cream cones and, by the end of 1934, $35 million worth of Disney character merchandise had been negotiated.

With the release of *The Band Concert* in 1935, sales dramatically increased; although Kamen vigilantly observed Disney's code of standards, including the stipulation that Mickey should never advertise cigars or cigarettes (although you *could* purchase a Mickey Mouse ash-tray), alcohol or drugs. One exception was when Mickey was allowed to endorse Scott and Bowne's cod-liver oil medicine, Scott's Emulsion, in Latin America where a great many children suffered from rickets.

The money received from merchandising helped finance the Studio's film production, but Mickey also helped many of the companies he worked with. In 1932, almost the entire population of the small New York town of Norwich were employed by the Norwich Knitting Company. The firm had closed down several of its textile mills but then it signed a contract with Disney to produce Mickey Mouse sweatshirts and, by 1935, was selling over one million of them a year.

Another contract was signed in 1933 with Ingersoll-Waterbury Company to produce Mickey Mouse watches. Ingersoll was on the brink of bankruptcy, but when the watch appeared (originally priced at

In 1935, the Lionel Corporation, which had made the original Mickey Mouse hand-car, produced a circus train with a tent decorated with pictures of Mickey and his friends.

$3.75 for a wristwatch and $1.50 for a pocket watch), it proved a phenomenal success. Ingersoll had to increase its staff from 300 to 3000, and Macy's department store sold as many as 11,000 Mickey Mouse watches in a single day.

Between 1933 and 1939, Ingersoll-Waterbury sold a total of $4,771,490.96 of Disney merchandise – representing almost a quarter of a million dollars in royalties. In 1957, Walt was presented with the 25 millionth Mickey Mouse watch and they are still made today, although one of the original time-pieces might now cost $400.

Another company whose flagging fortunes were revived by Mickey was the Lionel Corporation, which went into receivership in May 1934 with liquid assets of just $62,000 and liabilities of $296,000. Two months later, Lionel won a licence from Kamen to produce a Mickey Mouse hand-car. This clockwork tin toy had a Mickey and Minnie who worked the handles up and down and a circle of track for them to ride around on. The hand-car cost $1, and, within four months, 253,000 sets had been sold. By December, Lionel had paid its liabilities in full and, the following month, reported a profit.

Because of its association with Mickey, Lionel soon had 65 per cent of America's toy train business, and went on to produce various other Disney trains, including a circus train and another hand-car, with Santa Claus at the handle and a Mickey Mouse riding in his toy sack.

In 1984, a replica of the first Mickey Mouse hand-car (cast in "hi-strength polyester") was made, and sold for $199 – almost 200 times its original price.

Mouse merchandising has always been diverse: in 1934 Cartier's, the jewellers, were producing diamond-studded Mickey Mouse pins, while, in England, the confectionary firm of E. Sharp & Sons introduced a Mickey Mouse toffee – and sold 150 tons in a week.

Following Mickey's hey-day in the

1930s, Disney merchandise expanded to feature Donald Duck, Snow White, Pinocchio, Dumbo and many other characters, but the Mouse is still used – on toys, games, records, clothes, toiletries and foodstuffs – as well as appearing on merchandise inspired by TV's Mickey Mouse Club and on souvenirs from Disneyland, Walt Disney World and Tokyo Disneyland.

One thing is certain, for every item of Mickey memorabilia, there is somebody, somewhere, ready and willing to give it a home – even if it is something as unlikely as a talking Mickey Mouse pillow which squeaks: "Wanta have a picnic? You bring the cheese."

The cover of the book *Mickey Mouse and his Horse Tanglefoot,* one of the most popular of Mickey's adventures, published in 1936 by David McKay.

MOUSE BOOKS AND COMICS

When it was first rumoured in 1934 that Mickey Mouse could look forward to a promising career in comic strips instead of films, the *New York Sun* claimed they knew the reason why; "Consider the evidence," they said "look at the recent Mickey Mouse cartoons and see how they are failing in invention beside the increasing richness and fertility of the Symphonies." This was, in fact, rather unfair. Mickey's popularity with audiences was on the increase, and the Silly Symphonies did, after all, have the advantage of Technicolor.

But it was undeniable that the Mickey Mouse newspaper strip was strengthening its hold on the American public. In November 1929, at a request from King Features, Walt Disney had sent the first specimens, and even though the contract wasn't signed until 24 January 1930, the first strip appeared in *The New York Mirror* on 13 January. All the early Mickey Mouse strips were written by Walt Disney, drawn by Ub Iwerks, who actually received credit on the title, and inked by Win Smith. Shortly afterwards, however, Iwerks left to

form his own company, and Smith took over the drawing. But from 5 May 1930 until his retirement in 1975, Floyd Gottfredson, who had joined the studio to train as an animator, took on the task of drawing Mickey Mouse. Given the Mickey Mouse strip for what he thought would be a matter of a few months, he soon realized, as he was to admit later, "Walt just never got around to replacing me."

Throughout January and February 1930, the Mickey Mouse strips were a series of unconnected gags. The first continuous adventure, starring Mickey and Minnie in a story entitled *Mickey Mouse in Death Valley,* began on 31 March 1930. This also introduced Clarabelle Cow, Horace Horsecollar and Sylvester Shyster the lawyer; by 14 April Peg Leg Pete had arrived.

Many of Mickey's early adventures were more exciting and heroic than some of his on-screen appearances. As Bill Blackbeard, founder of the San Francisco Academy of Comic Art, noted: "It was a death-defying, tough, steel-gutted Mickey Mouse, quite unlike the mild, blandly benign Mouse of contemporary Disney Studio usage, who held the kids of 1933 rapt with his adventures on pirate dirigibles, cannibal islands and bullet-tattered fighter planes."

Peg Leg Pete's popularity as the comic

Between 1933 and 1955, a number of different writers worked on the Mickey Mouse daily strip. Both the Sunday pages illustrated below were penned by Merrill de Maris and inked by Ted Thwaites.

One of the rarest and most eagerly collected of Mickey Mouse books, the *Mickey Mouse Waddle Book* was published by Blue Ribbon Books, Inc., New York, in 1934. The book contained walking, cut-out models of Mickey, Minnie, Pluto and Tanglefoot, as well as the ramp and brass hinges needed to assemble the display.

strips' arch villain even led to the character regaining his missing leg, because Gottfredson kept forgetting on which side the peg leg was supposed to be drawn. Donald Duck, who went to even greater fame under the penmanship of Carl Barks, first appeared in *Mickey Mouse Runs His Own Newspaper* (1935), and Dippy (later Goofy) in *Mickey Mouse the Detective* (1933-4).

Floyd Gottfredson continued writing the comic strip as well as illustrating it until 1932, when he decided to bring in other writers. Up until 1955, Webb Smith, Ted Osborne, Merrill de Maris, Dick Shaw and Bill Walsh adapted Gottfredson's original plots into script form. (Bill Walsh later produced the *Mickey Mouse Club* and *Mary Poppins*.) In 1932, the first colour Mickey Mouse strip appeared in a Sunday newspaper, three years before Mickey starred in his first Technicolor film, *The Band Concert*.

Such was the success of the Mickey Mouse strip that betwen the years 1930 and 1966 it was featured in a total of 113 papers. It was also reported, during the mid-1930s, that the strip was read daily by over 28 million people. In November 1933, a *Mickey Mouse Magazine* was launched on behalf of a chain of dairies to advertise milk products, and in 1935 Kay Kamen published the first issue of his *Mickey Mouse Magazine*. During

the 1940s it changed its title to *Walt Disney's Comics and Stories*, and these were continued in Dell and Gold Key comic books until the late 1970s, all titles being published by the Western Publishing Company. By this time, a wealth of other Disney characters appeared in the comic format, some, like Uncle Scrooge, drawn by Carl Barks, making their début there.

As the Mouse gathered momentum around the world, local artists contributed to foreign versions of Mickey and his pals. He became known as Topolino in Italy, Micky Maus in Germany, Miku Maous in Greece, Miki Eger in Hungary, El Raton Miguelito in South America, Mic-Kay in Vietnam, Miki Tikus in Indonesia, Mi Lao Shu in China and Musse Pigg in Sweden. Many of these comics used Gottfredson's American strip under licence. The French *Le Journal de Mickey* started life in 1934 and is still published today, and in the early 1940s, the French publishers Hachette produced some of the early American strips in book form, including the titles such as *Mickey Pirate, Mickey Jockey* and *Mickey Detective*.

In Britain, *Mickey Mouse Weekly* began life in November 1936, with glorious colour covers drawn by Wilfred Haughton. The first issue sold 375,000 copies, a number that increased to over 600,000 copies a week. In his first letter to readers, Mickey introduced the new comic by saying "Dear

Folks, Here it is at last . . . the Very First Issue of my Very Own Paper! And it's what the fire irons called the kitchen range, isn't it . . . Just Grate!" Special articles throughout the comic included "Clara Cluck's Kookery Korner," "Goofy Gossip," and "The Mickey Mouse Club News." Just as Mickey had done in the early American *Mickey Mouse Magazine,* he would often advertise such household items as Post Toasties breakfast cereals and, in the popular *Mickey Mouse Annuals,* published in 1932 and drawn by Wilfred Haughton, Bovril Beef Extract, Kiwi Shoe Polish and Peak Frean's biscuits.

Since 1975, the newspaper Mickey strips have been written by Del Connell and drawn by Roman Arambula, while many of the vintage strips have been reprinted in book form.

Although a wealth of Mickey Mouse books is published today, that wasn't always the case. In fact, in 1929 Roy Disney had quite a problem persuading publishers to print books on Mickey at all. With the exception of *The Mickey Mouse Book* (1930), only David McKay of Philadelphia had the foresight to take up Roy's proposals, when, in 1931, he published *The Adventures of Mickey Mouse.* A giant Mickey Mouse colouring book followed from the Saalfield Publishing Company and, by the mid-1930s, Blue Ribbon Books of New York had launched a successful series of pop-ups on Mickey, Minnie and some of the Silly Symphonies. 1931 also saw the publication of *Mickey Mouse's Movie Stories Volume One,* followed in 1934 by *Volume Two,* each featuring numerous black and white illustrations from the films, and two years later saw the publication of one of the best known Mickey stories, *Mickey Mouse and his Horse Tanglefoot.*

Perhaps the most collectible item, however, was the unique *Mickey Mouse Waddle Book,* published in 1934. Retailing for a dollar, it contained press-out, three-dimensional cardboard figures that actually walked. It is highly sought after as one of the early examples of the mechanical book.

In 1935, the 10-year-old King of Siam accepted as a gift from Walt Disney several Mickey Mouse books. He was a great fan of the Mouse, and 25 years later he repaid Walt's kindness by bestowing on him the "most noble order of the Crown."

Among more recent additions to Mickey's library has been the *Mickey Mouse Cook Book,* featuring a recipe for Mickey's Sugar Biscuits, and other exotic dishes including Pluto's Hotdogs and Cinderella's Melted Cheese Sandwich. Mickey's popularity in print has never waned and shows no sign of doing so. Looking back, in 1984, on the little character whose personality he helped create, Floyd Gottfredson said: "Mickey was my very exciting and satisfying companion for nearly forty-six years. And he is still very much alive and well."

Opposite above: A regular feature of the Mickey Mouse Club was Mousekartoon Time, during which classic Mickey Mouse films, such as *Mickey's Trailer* (1938), were screened.

WHO'S THE LEADER OF THE CLUB?

Who's the leader of the club
That's made for you and me?
M-I-C-K-E-Y
M-O-U-S-E.

For five nights a week, for four years from 1955, over 12 million American children tuned in to ABC-TV and sang along with this famous *Mickey Mouse Club* theme song.

But it was not the first Mickey Mouse Club, nor was the Mousemania it unleashed an entirely new phenomenon. In September 1929, Harry W. Woodin, Manager of the Fox Dome Theatre in Ocean Park, California, had approached Disney with an idea for starting a children's cinema club. Disney readily gave the project his blessing and the first Mickey Mouse Club came into being.

The Club was an immediate success; and Disney invited Harry Woodin to leave his job and come to the Studio as General Manager of Mickey Mouse Clubs. Woodin worked hard and, by the end of 1930, there were hundreds of Clubs meeting every Saturday in cinemas all over America. Within two years no fewer than a million youngsters were enrolled: a figure which equalled the American membership of the Scout movement.

The two main functions of the Mickey Mouse Club, as Harry Woodin defined them, early in 1930, were: first "to provide an easily arranged and inexpensive method of getting and holding the patronage of youngsters"; and, second, "through inspirational, patriotic, and character-building activities related to the Club, to aid children in learning good citizenship."

"There were also," wrote Cecil Munsey, "the unspoken purposes of making Mickey Mouse cartoons more popular and promoting character merchandise."

Cinema managers paid a license fee of $25 a year to run a club, but any costs incurred were invariably off-set by sponsorship from local trades-people – particularly those with Mickey Mouse goods for sale. The clubs met at lunchtime matinees, some theatres using official club currency of "Ten Scents" (of cheese) to pay for admission, and the programme included, in addition to Mickey Mouse cartoons, a suitable feature film and a serial.

There was a club password, a secret hand-shake and a highly elaborate ritual to be observed at all meetings. After an opening cartoon, the club's officials (who were chosen from the members and changed every eight weeks) took their places on the cinema's stage. Ranged in a semi-circle would be a Chief Mickey Mouse, a Chief Minnie Mouse, a Master of Ceremonies, a Cheerleader, a Songleader, two Sergeants-at-Arms, a Colour-bearer and a Courier, each of whom wore a Mickey Mouse Club Officer Button and a specially designed vest (waistcoat) and fez.

Friday on the Mickey Mouse Club was Talent Roundup Day. Here Sharon Baird heads the Mouseketeers for a hoe-down routine.

Then the Chief Mickey Mouse would read the Club Creed, which was printed on the back of every membership card:

I will be a squareshooter in my home, in school, on the playgrounds, wherever I may be.

I will be truthful and honourable and strive always to make myself a better and more useful little citizen.

I will respect my elders and help the aged, the helpless and children smaller than myself.

In short, I will be a good American!

To which Club members responded with the Mickey Mouse Club pledge: "Mickey Mice do not SWEAR – SMOKE – CHEAT or LIE." The American flag was then brought on stage and the audience sang a verse of "America."

These formalities were followed by a variety of club activities: games, stunts and contests, after which everyone joined in the Club Yell:

HANDY! DANDY!
SWEET AS CANDY!
HAPPY KIDS ARE WE!
EENIE! ICKIE!
MINNIE! MICKEY!
M-O-U-S-E!

Finally, before the movies were screened, the members all sang along with the Club's Theme Song, "Minnie's Yoo-Hoo."

It wasn't long before there were Mickey Mouse Clubs meeting all over the world. Mickey had a particularly strong following in Britain, where the first Club was founded in 1933 at Darlington's Arcade Cinema; within just four years there were over 200 British

Jimmie Dodd and Roy Williams, whose ebullient personalities made the Mickey Mouse Club television show into a daily institution.

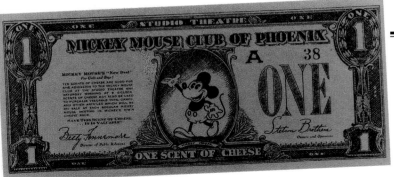

The early Mickey Mouse Clubs met in local cinemas, and members had their own "currency" like this "One Scent of Cheese" bill, which was used by the Mickey Mouse Club of Phoenix, Arizona.

Clubs. In December 1937, *The New York Times Magazine* reported that there was even a Mickey Mouse Club in Singapore, and the paper's correspondent speculated whether Mickey was simply "waiting patiently for the collapse of civilization" in order to become "Emperor of the World."

In America, however, the Studio was finding it increasingly difficult to administer so many clubs, and in 1935, therefore, it was decided to phase them out, although many continued to meet and one in Miami survived well into the 1950s.

But then, 25 years after its creation, the Mickey Mouse Club provided the inspiration for what became the most famous children's programme in the history of television.

Walt Disney was the first Hollywood producer to recognize the potential of the new medium of television, and to look for ways of using it. His first TV show had been aired on Christmas Day 1950, and, four years later, he launched his first television series, *Disneyland*, on ABC. The show was designed to preview – and, later, to help promote – the Disneyland theme-park being built in Anaheim.

Disneyland proved a very expensive project and one of the corporations that financed it was the American Broadcasting Company. As part of Disney's deal with ABC, and because of the success of the *Disneyland* series, the Studio agreed to produce a daily children's television show. For a format, Disney went back to the ideas used in the Mickey Mouse Clubs of the 1930s, and he offered his old friend Mickey,

who had now effectively retired from movie-making, the job of being host on the new show.

The Mickey Mouse Club went into production with Bill Walsh (who had written many of the Mouse's comic-strip adventures) as producer.

It was decided that the Mickey Mouse Club should be presented by children, so, together with Bill Walsh, Disney auditioned thousands of hopefuls, finally choosing 24 youngsters, many of whom, over the next few years, became stars of the small screen: Darlene, Bobby, Sharon, Lonnie, Cubby and Karen and the young lady who became the heart-throb of millions of American boys – Annette Funicello.

To accompany the children, who were known as Mouseketeers, Disney selected two adult co-stars: Jimmie Dodd and Roy Williams. Jimmie Dodd was a song-writer who had composed for the *Disneyland* TV show, as well as a talented singer, dancer and actor. Dodd's strong Christian beliefs gave his contributions to the Mickey Mouse Club a simple morality that Disney liked and parents approved of, and that inspired the Club's improving Mousethoughts and such songs as "Do What the Good Book Says."

Roy Williams, who became known as the Big Mouseketeer, was a large, genial cartoonist and gag-man who had worked on many Disney films. He designed the Mouseketeers' hat – a black skull-cap with mouse ears – inspired by a gag in an early

Mickey Mouse film, *The Karnival Kid,* in which Mickey had raised the top of his head to Minnie as if it were a hat.

And then there was Mickey. An illuminated Broadway theatre sign flashed the opening credits – "Walt Disney and Mickey Mouse present MICKEY MOUSE CLUB" – and the Mouse appeared, together with many of his old gang, in the show's lively title-sequence with its un-forgettable "Mickey Mouse March," which became a classic of 1950s American culture.

The Mickey Mouse Club was screened Monday to Friday for four years from 3 October 1955. Each day had a different theme and was introduced by Mickey wearing a different costume. Monday was "Fun with Music Day" and Mickey appeared in the boater and striped blazer of a song-and-dance man. "Hi, Mouseketeers!" he would squeak, "Big doings this week – adventure, fun, music, cartoons, news . . . Everybody ready? Then on with the show!"

Tuesday was "Guest Star Day" and Mickey dressed up in bow-tie and tails; and Wednesday was "Stunt Day" (also known as "Anything Can Happen Day"), for which

Mickey, wearing his Sorcerer's Apprentice costume, arrived on a flying-carpet. Thursday was "Circus Day," when Mickey donned the uniform and plumed hat of a band-leader. Finally there was Friday's Show, with Mickey dressed in Western Gear and twirling a lasso to introduce "Talent Roundup Day."

In the *Mickey Mouse Club Annual* (1956), Walt Disney wrote: "Everyone who regularly watches the Mickey Mouse Club Television Show is automatically a member of the Mickey Mouse Club and a Mouseketeer First-Class in good standing." Thousands of children bought their own set of Mouseketeer-ears (price 69 cents), sat on Mickey Mouse Club Stools to watch the TV show, ate their suppers off Mickey Mouse dinner sets and tried to play the "Mousegetar" – just as Jimmie did. They learnt all the words in the "Mouseka-Dictionary" ("MOUSEKAMIXER – *used for making Mousekamalts*"; "MOUSEKAPLAY – *Fairplay, playing with others cheerfully*") and always joining in the Mickey Mouse Alma Mater:

M-I-C
See you real soon!
K-E-Y
Why? Because we like you!
M-O-U-S-E.

The Mickey Mouse club ran as an hour show for two years (1955-7), and then in a half-hour format (1957-9). Later it was re-released in syndication and shown in many foreign countries including Finland, France, Italy, Switzerland, Mexico and Japan. And thirty years after its premiere, the Mouse Club became a regular feature of the Disney Channel.

In 1977, the New Mickey Mouse Club was launched, with 12 new Mouseketeers in snappy modern costumes (Mickey himself sported a jumpsuit), and a decidedly rock tempo to the show's music. At the age of almost fifty Mickey once again took on a new lease of life.

MICKEY'S
NEW LEASE OF LIFE

THE HOST WITH THE MOST

In Anaheim, California, on 17 July 1985, Disneyland – Walt Disney's greatest dream – celebrated its 30th birthday. Fireworks exploded in a myriad of colours around the turrets of the Sleeping Beauty Castle, and, while the brass bands played, thousands of people cheered the glittering array of guest stars invited especially for the event. On Main Street USA, the gateway to the "Happiest Place on Earth," Disneyland's official host Mickey Mouse headed the parade on top of a giant pink birthday cake, smiling and waving at his countless fans, as he has done at every parade since 1955.

In fact, Walt Disney's idea for Disneyland began in the early 1940s. While the Mouse was achieving worldwide acclaim and the Studio was concentrating on feature-length animated films, Disney was already thinking about an amusement park adjacent to his Burbank Studio. But the Second World War intervened and prevented the "magical little park," as it was called by employees around the Studio, from ever reaching fruition.

In the early 1950s, however, Disney once again took up the idea of an amusement park and saw the new medium, television, as a possible source of finance. Unlike other Hollywood producers who could only see television as a threat to their industry Walt embarked on a series of programmes entitled *Disneyland* for the American Broadcasting Company (ABC). In return, Disney requested that ABC help finance the building of Disneyland.

The television series began on 27 October 1954. By the time Disneyland opened, in the July of the following year, it already boasted one of the biggest and most spectacular advertising campaigns ever launched. Backed by a live, coast-to-coast

A smiling Mickey Mouse poses in front of the Sleeping Beauty Castle at Disneyland park in California.

Right: When Roy Disney dedicated the opening of Walt Disney World in Florida in 1971 to his brother Walt's memory, Mickey joined him on the podium to help launch the festivities.

television spectacular, Disneyland was an overnight sensation.

The core of Disneyland is Fantasyland, at the centre of which stands the Sleeping Beauty Castle. From here "guests" in 1955 could visit the park's other themed environments – Adventureland, Frontierland, Main Street USA and Tomorrowland. Ever since the drawbridge of the castle was lowered "in honour of the children of the World," Mickey and the gang have led a steady stream of youngsters across the moat and into the history books.

In the months that followed, Mickey invited to Disneyland his many pals from the *Mickey Mouse Club*. The streets were full of cheering Mouseketeers, while club star Roy Williams often sat in Tomorrowland drawing portraits of Mickey and his chums under the banner "Walt Disney Characters Drawn While You Wait." Over the next few years, a number of new attractions were added to Disneyland and the park was visited regularly by many famous celebrities including film stars, politicians and royalty.

When on 17 June 1971 a payroll clerk from New Jersey became the 100 millionth visitor to Disneyland, Mickey was present to welcome her and launch a summer-long celebration. Later that year he flew to

Orlando, Florida, to help Roy Disney with the grand opening of Walt Disney World, dedicated to the memory of Walt. Now Mickey was host to two amusement destinations, but Minnie would often help him with the workload. In a Studio interview, when asked if he saw much of his sweetheart, Mickey replied "We're both so busy these days. We never seem to be in the same place at the same time. When I'm at Disneyland, in California, it always seems like she's at Walt Disney World in Florida."

But Mickey found himself spending more and more time at Walt Disney World. Unlike Disneyland, which is set in a cramped city near Los Angeles, Orlando offered a vast area of open land on which to build. Apart from a "Magic Kingdom," Disney World's 43 square miles also consist of the Fort Wilderness Camp Ground, River Country, Discovery Island, golf courses, a

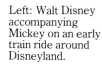

Left: Walt Disney accompanying Mickey on an early train ride around Disneyland.

Shopping Village, a Hotel Plaza and EPCOT Center, an exciting showcase of tomorrow and permanent world's fair. Mickey has found time to appear in all these places. His film career was a cinch in comparison. He even had the opportunity to conduct an orchestra comprised of his many friends in "The Mickey Mouse Revue," which featured music from Mickey's favourite Walt Disney films and proved to be a very popular attraction with visitors. "The Mickey Mouse Revue" was brought to life by a sophisticated system of robotics controlled by computer tape, first designed by Disney "Imagineers" for Disneyland in 1963 and known as Audio-Animatronics.

For America's Bicentennial in 1976, Mickey headed the spectacular costume parade on Main Street, and when the world's most famous Mouse turned fifty, in 1978, he braved the risk of severe jet-lag rushing from California to Florida to take part in his own birthday celebrations coast-to-coast.

Mickey's costume in the parks has changed throughout the years. When he appeared in Disneyland's opening celebrations he wore the outfit in which he began his film career. But as the years progressed and his responsibilities increased, he started to wear his official tail coat and long red trousers – though still supported by two shiny buttons. When, in 1985, Mickey made his first appearance at EPCOT Center (Experimental Prototype Community of Tomorrow) he and Minnie had already entered the space age. They wore silver moon suits as Mousetronauts when appearing in Future World, EPCOT Center's equivalent of tomorrowland. However EPCOT also comprises microcosms of various countries of the world, including Japan, France, Morocco and the United Kingdom. As international host, Mickey has appeared in Chinese style finery while his pal Goofy was once spotted in a kilt.

Mickey is so proud of EPCOT Center that he has joined the ranks of the educators. In a special comic book Mickey takes Goofy on a voyage of discovery around one of Future World's scientific pavilions – The Universe of Energy – exploring mankind's need to harness natural sources of power such as Solar Energy.

MODERN MOUSE

Hollywood is a city responsible for creating legends and many of the famous names can be seen as gold stars on the pavement of Hollywood Boulevard's Walk of Fame. When, on 18 November 1978, Mickey Mouse joined the personalities of television and film whose names are immortalized in concrete, he was the first cartoon character to have done so. Mickey was there because Hollywood and the world in general were celebrating his 50th birthday. The razzmatazz that surrounded this noble event put the half-century celebrations of a majority of Mickey's human counterparts in the shade.

In conjunction with the National Broadcasting Company (NBC), Walt Disney Productions presented Mickey in a celebratory television spectacular, as part of the long-running series *The Wonderful World of Disney*. Among the real-life stars invited along to help Mickey shrug off five decades of movie history and prepare himself for five more were James Stewart, Burt Reynolds, Gregory Peck, Sally Field, Bob Hope, Annette Funicello, Billy Graham and even Kermit the Frog, who boasted a close friendship with the world's most famous mouse. "It'll be Mickey's show," producer Phil May had promised, and everything will be geared towards Mickey. He's a universal personality. He transcends politics and ethnic barriers, but on his own level he overcomes the day-to-day problems we all face and he does it with a smile."

And across the globe, friends and admirers of Mickey smiled back. At Disneyland in Anaheim, any visitor who, on arriving at the park entrance, discovered that his birthday fell in the same year as Mickey's (1928), was granted free admission and unlimited use of all the Disneyland attractions. The special celebration lasted for two days. At 2.00 p.m. there

When Tokyo Disneyland opened, in spring 1983, Mickey sent his "Mickey Mouse Revue" to Japan as a special gift. He even took time off to appear there in person, dressed in traditional Japanese costume. It was natural therefore, when duty called, that he offered to fly "around the world in 30 days" to celebrate Disneyland's 30th Anniversary. Accompanied by the Park's Ambassador, Melissa Tyler, he set off on 13 February 1985, stopping over in Tokyo, Peking, Singapore, New Delhi, Berlin, Budapest, Geneva, Paris, Rome and Rio de Janeiro. He has been so much a part of Walt Disney's wonderful Magic Kingdoms, that it seemed fitting that, during the Disneyland 30th Anniversary television spectacular, actress Julie Andrews should have summed up everyone's feelings about Mickey and Disneyland, by wishing them both a Happy Birthday.

Mickey stands in front of an early painting of EPCOT Center in Walt Disney World for his 50th birthday portrait by Disney artist and designer John Hench.

As part of his 50th birthday celebrations, Mickey, accompanied by Minnie, stopped off in Disneyland and Walt Disney World to visit the Main Street cinema for a special screening of his first film appearance, *Steamboat Willie*, made in 1928.

was a special parade in honour of Mickey, a cake-cutting ceremony in front of the Sleeping Beauty Castle, a show at the Golden Horseshoe Revue in Frontierland and free access to the Fantasyland Theater, which screened classic Mickey Mouse cartoons all day long. At 2.45 p.m. an announcement rang out across Disneyland: "Wherever you are in the Park, please pause and join us in singing 'Happy Birthday' to our favorite mouse."

NBC's prestigious *Saturday Night Live* show played host to Mickey for a special guest appearance. The Franklin Mint produced a 24-carat gold on sterling silver pendant to mark Mickey's birthday. This limited-edition collectors' item was, the publicity handout explained, "For anyone who's ever run off to Disneyland . . . worn a Mickey Mouse watch . . . or simply wanted to!"; and in Washington D.C., the Library of Congress launched a major exhibition called "Building A Better Mouse" in honour of Mickey. Even the speakers at the House of Representatives discussed Mickey's birthday: "It is, therefore, appropriate for this House to extend best birthday wishes to an entity which has a perfect political rating. Mickey and his goofy friends."

Washington D.C. was, in fact, only one of the stops on Mickey's cross-country

whistle-stop tour. Accompanied by animator Ward Kimball, Mickey's special Amtrak train left Los Angeles on 13 November and visited some 57 cities before arriving in New York on 18 November, exactly 50 years from his début in 1928. A commemorative plaque was installed at the Broadway Theater (formerly the Colony) to mark it as the site of his official birthplace. Breakfast was served to a happy legion of fans, before they filed into the theatre to watch a special screening of *Steamboat Willie*, followed by a full celebrity programme.

With just a hint of the fun to come, Mickey posed next to a model of EPCOT Center for artist John Hench, who said: "The Mouse that started it all once again leads the way with a panoramic preview of our next frontier – EPCOT, the last and greatest of Walt Disney's dreams." It was pointed out that a close inspection of the portrait reveals "a few subtle strokes of grey above Mickey's eyes and cheeks," but Hench makes no comment except to say, "Mickey was, and is, something of Walt's. He came to stand for Walt Disney Productions and for all of our achievements. And now he is pointing our way to the future."

But Mickey's 50th birthday celebrations

were only the culmination of his popularity around the world. Apart from being a host at the Disney theme parks, he guest-starred in the arena spectaculars *Disney on Parade*, two of which toured Europe during 1972 and 1975, and also in ice shows. In the late 1970s Mickey appeared on films and video. His most "memorable moments" were made available to the home-movie enthusiast and his life story appeared on a special Disneyland album. Ovation Records in America released a boxed set of famous Disney soundtrack excerpts featuring a cover picture of Mickey conducting. During 1982, *Fantasia* was re-released giving audiences a chance to see Mickey perform as the Sorcerer's Apprentice to a new, digitally-recorded version of Dukas's music by veteran Disney musician, Irwin Kostal.

On television he teamed up with his pals, Donald, Goofy and Pluto in a series of 26 weekly instalments of *Mickey and Donald*, featuring some of his classic routines. He arrived on video in England in November 1981 with *Mickey's Golden Jubilee*, while in America, a number of Mickey's classic cartoons were released in the limited Gold Edition collectors' series, with introductions by stars such as Annette Funicello, Hayley Mills and Donald Pleasence, and costing a mere $30 a piece.

After the first Disney stamp was issued in the USA in 1968, honoring Walt Disney, the Intergovernmental Philatelic Corporation of New York was licensed, in 1979, by Walt Disney Productions to produce an extensive range of Disney character stamps. Mickey appeared as sportsman in Grenada and proudly went fishing on the Turks & Caicos Islands stamps. He was a mailman in the Republic of Maldives, a piano player in the Commonwealth of Dominica and, for the 10th Anniversary of the moonwalk, in St. Lucia Mickey and the gang dressed in spacesuits and took a voyage of discovery across the moon's surface. Some stamps have even featured Mickey's friends from

the beginning of his career, including Horace Horsecollar and Clarabelle Cow.

In 1952, Walt Disney Productions set up a company with the specific purpose of supplying educational material for schools. By the 1980s, the Walt Disney Educational Media Company – WDEMCO as it is known – used Mickey as the symbol of its teaching abilities. In some cartoons Mickey advised Goofy on such issues as how to spend his money wisely, and his classic adventures including *Thru the Mirror*, *Mickey's Trailer*, *Steamboat Willie*, *The Band Concert*, and *The Sorcerer's Apprentice* have been used in a variety of educational ways.

A new-look Mickey in Stars and Stripes, reflecting on his early days, as captured in this amusing illustration by veteran Disney animator, Ward Kimball.

With the importance of computers in education, students were encouraged to develop essential grammar and spelling skills with the Atari computer game, *Mickey in the Great Outdoors*. WDEMCO co-developed *Mickey's Space Adventure* with California software company Sierra On-Line, an adventure game about the Solar System.

One of Mickey's most important roles has been hosting The Disney Channel, a pay-TV network, which started life on 18 April 1983 at 7.00 a.m., with a show entitled "Good Morning, Mickey." Mickey introduced audiences to aerobics in *Mousercise*, set in his own health club and illustrating the importance of physical fitness as inspired by his successful record album. He even offered his services as the Channel's symbol and could be seen wearing his Sorcerer's Apprentice outfit in all publicity.

Although it's not even 10 years since Mickey's 50th birthday, he has achieved more in that time in various areas of entertainment than any other celebrity, whether as a new disco-star, television host or educator. His popularity knows no limits, as *Sunday Times* reporter, Tony Osman, discovered when he researched experiments that suggest animals may be instinctively capable of aesthetic appreciation. When discussing a monkey's response to images on screen, he wrote, "An unfamiliar animal could hold his interest for minutes, and he would watch a Mickey Mouse movie for as long as the film continued."

As John Hench once noted: "I've always seen Mickey as a dynamic, busy fellow, looking with exuberance toward the next pioneering achievement. Perhaps that is one of the ways he is closest to Walt."

Mickey followed in the steps of John Travolta when, in 1979, he recorded *Mickey Mouse Disco*, featuring such numbers as "Mousetrap" and "Macho Duck."

BACK IN FRONT OF THE CAMERAS

In the spring of 1982, Hollywood was a-buzz with rumour and speculation. "Guess who is making a comeback?" asked the *Daily News* on 5 April, "Mickey Mouse, that's who."

The idea of bringing Mickey out of retirement and putting him back in front of the cameras came from Disney animator, Burny Mattinson. Although Mattinson had never worked with the Mouse (he joined the studio in 1953, the year Mickey made his last movie), he had an affection for the little character and sensed that the time was ripe for his return to the silver screen: "People would constantly ask me, 'When are *they* going to bring back Mickey and the gang?' Finally, I realized that 'they' was me. My wife (also a Disney animator) told me to stop talking and start doing."

In 1981, Mattinson had come across a Disney record album, made in 1974, which featured Mickey and his friends in a musical play based on Charles Dickens's *A Christmas Carol*. The subject seemed an ideal one for a film treatment, and Mattinson submitted a proposal to the Studio's president, who liked the idea and gave the project the go-ahead.

Mickey was to be cast as Bob Cratchit, the overworked, underpaid employee of the miserly Ebenezer Scrooge: a role well-suited to his good-natured, long-suffering personality. The part of Scrooge, the "squeezing, wrenching, grasping, scraping, clutching, covetous old sinner," went to Donald Duck's uncle, Scrooge McDuck, who had achieved international fame as a Disney comic-book character.

Goofy was signed to portray the Ghost of Jacob Marley (although, *being* Goofy, he was to play the part for laughs rather than for terror). Guest-starring as the spirits of Christmas Past, Present and Yet to Come were Pinocchio's diminutive conscience, Jiminy Cricket, Willie the Giant (from "Mickey and the Beanstalk") and Mickey's long-time enemy, Pete.

Other members of Mickey's old gang were given supporting roles – Minnie Mouse as Mrs. Cratchit, two of Mickey's nephews and a niece, as the Cratchit children, Donald Duck (in a curiously benign mood) as Scrooge's kindly nephew, and Daisy Duck as Isabel the lost love of Scrooge's youth. Cameo appearances were to be made by, among others, Clarabelle Cow, Horace Horsecollar and Clara Cluck; Toad, Rat, Mole and Badger (from *The Wind in the Willows*), the Three Little Pigs and the Big Bad Wolf.

Although Scrooge was, undoubtedly, the film's central character, the movie was to be called *Mickey's Christmas Carol*; and the familiar pre-credit sequence card of Mickey's head against a background of radiating light was to be used again for the

first time in 30 years – amended, however, to show Mickey in a top hat and muffler.

As producer and director of the 25-minute film, Burny Mattinson faced a number of problems, not least of which was that none of the Studio's animators had ever worked with Mickey and the gang, and the artists had to learn techniques of character animation that had not been used for years. They soon discovered that the most difficult character to draw was Mickey, who was to be animated in the style of his appearance in *Fantasia*.

The task of making Mickey move went to Mark Henn, a young animator who hadn't even been born when Mickey gave his farewell screen performance. "He has a certain look," Henn told an interviewer, "and if he isn't drawn quite right – if his nose is too big or his ears are in the wrong position – it will be very obvious."

There was also the question of Mickey's voice. Jimmy Macdonald, who had taken over as Mickey's spokesman from Walt

Disney, was now retired, and a new voice had to be found. The role was assumed by sound editor Wayne Allwine.

Mickey's Christmas Carol was released in December 1983, and it was a great success. Mickey's acting was as vivacious as ever; his fur didn't show so much as a hint of grey; and he looked much younger and trimmer than he had in his last film in 1953.

His portrayal of Bob Cratchit was widely – and rightly – praised, and, it is rumoured, we haven't yet seen the last of Mickey Mouse on screen.

And so, the Mickey Mouse story goes on. But what is the secret of his undying appeal?

It is a question people have been wrestling with now for almost sixty years. As early as 1933, the American playwright, Arthur Miller wrote: "Mickey is 'Everyman', battling for life and love . . . he is honest, decent, a good sportsman . . . Mickey has his little weaknesses, but there is no question which side he is on. He is little David who slays Goliath. He is that most popular, because more universally conceivable, hero – the little man who shuts his eyes and pastes the big bully in the jaw."

The same year, Walt Disney wrote in the *Overland Monthly* that his films were made for "the Mickey audience . . . it has no racial, national, political, religious or social differences or affiliations; the Mickey audience is made up of parts of people, of that deathless, precious, ageless, absolutely primitive remnant of something in every world-wracked human being which makes us play with children's toys and laugh without self-consciousness at silly things, and sing in bathtubs, and dream and believe that our babies are uniquely beautiful. You know . . . the Mickey in us."

Forty years later, in 1975, veteran Disney animator Marc Davis said that Mickey Mouse was "one of the greatest folk characters of all time . . . I don't think

Left: A scene from *Mickey's Christmas Carol* featured on Walt Disney Productions' 1933 Christmas card.
Below: Mickey Mouse and his creator became internationally known; even in this early photograph, Mickey was already on top of the world.

From Christmas past

you can name any character that represents the last fifty years better than Mickey . . . He's a completely symbolical guy."

If Mickey *is* a symbol, then he symbolizes many different things to different people. To artists, he has long been one of the most compelling symbols of 20th-century culture, a pop icon. For Andy Warhol, Mickey was as significant an image as Marilyn or the Campbell's soup-can; and Ernest Trova, who made a number of Mickey sculptures, once observed that the three most powerful graphic images of this century were the swastika, the Coca-Cola bottle and the ever-smiling face of Mickey Mouse.

To Walt Disney, Mickey was "a symbol of independence." Writing for *Who's Who in Hollywood*, in 1948, he said that Mickey had "popped out of my mind onto a drawing pad at a time when . . . disaster seemed just around the corner." Disney never forgot the debt he owed Mickey and would often remark: "I hope we never lose sight of one fact . . . that this was all started by a Mouse."

Today, Mickey is still a symbol of the Company he helped to found: his likeness appears on Walt Disney Company

letterheads, Christmas cards and canteen menus; one of the roads in the Studio, at Burbank, is called Mickey Avenue and the Studio's post office has a Mickey Mouse-shaped mail-box.

The famous mouse-ears are featured on a variety of corporate insignia: on an aeroplane for the Disney Travel Company; on a mortar-board for the Walt Disney Educational Media Company; and as lines on a TV screen for The Disney Channel. Most significantly they are found sprouting from the top of a globe as the logo for Walt Disney World; the entire planet it suggests, now belongs to the Mouse.

"All we ever intended for him or expected of him," his creator once said, "was that he should continue to make people everywhere chuckle with him and at him. We didn't burden him with any social symbolism, we made him no mouthpiece for frustration or harsh satire. Mickey was simply a little personality assigned to the purposes of laughter."

That was Mickey's job and he has done it, and is still doing it, faithfully and incomparably.

BIBLIOGRAPHY

Bailey, Adrian, *Walt Disney's World of Fantasy*, Everest House, New York; Paper Tiger, London, 1982

Bain, David and Harris, Bruce, *Mickey Mouse Fifty Happy Years*, Crown Publishers, Inc., New York; New English Library, London, 1977

Barks, Carl and Gottfredson, Floyd, *Two Disney Legends Share Their Memories*, Nemo magazine, June 1984

Barrier, Mike, *An Interview with Carl Stalling*, Funnyworld Magazine, 1971

Butcher, Harold, *An International Mouse*, New York Times, 28 October 1934

Canemaker, John, *Treasures of Disney Animation Art* (Introduction), Abbeville Press, New York, 1982

Carr, Harry, *The Only Unpaid Movie Star*, American Magazine, March 1931

Charlot, J., *Art from the Mayans to Disney*, Sheed and Ward, New York and London, 1939

Churchill, Douglas W., *Now Mickey Mouse Enters Art's Temple*, The New York Times Magazine, 3 June 1934

-- --, *Disney's Philosophy*, The New York Times Magazine, 6 March 1938

Culhane, John, *Walt Disney's Fantasia*, Harry N. Abrams, Inc., New York, 1983

-- --, *A Mouse For All Seasons*, Saturday Review, 11 November 1978

Disney, Walt, *The Cartoons Contribution to Children*, Overland Monthly, 1933

-- --, *The Life Story of Mickey Mouse*, Windsor, January 1934

-- --, *What Mickey Means to Me*, Who's Who in Hollywood, 1948

Eisen, A., *Two Disney Artists*, Crimmers: The Harvard Journal of Pictorial Fiction, 1975

Feild, Robert, D., *The Art of Walt Disney*, Macmillan, New York; Collins, London and Glasgow, 1942

Fidler, James, M., *A Mouse in a Million*, Screenland, February 1935

Finch, Christopher, *The Art of Walt Disney – From Mickey Mouse to the Magic Kingdoms*, Harry N. Abrams, Inc., New York, 1973

Fishwick, Marshall, *Aesop in Hollywood*, Saturday Review, 1954

Forster, E.M., *Mickey and Minnie*, The Spectator, 19 January 1934

Gottfredson, Floyd, *Walt Disney's Mickey Mouse; Best Comics*, Abbeville Press, New York, 1978

Gottfredson, Floyd and Andrae, Tom, *The Mouse's Other Master*, Nemo magazine, April 1984

Heide, Robert and Gilman, John, *Cartoon Collectibles*, Doubleday & Co., New York, 1983

Herbert, Russell, *L'Affaire Mickey Mouse*, The New York Times Magazine, 26 December 1937

Johnston, Alva, *Mickey Mouse*, Woman's Home Companion, July 1934

Keller, Keith, *The Mickey Mouse Club Scrapbook*, Grosset & Dunlap, Inc., New York, 1975

Lejeune, C.A., *Disney's Cartoons*, Cinema (London), 1931

Low, David, *Leonardo da Disney*, The New Republic, 5 January 1942

Maltin, Leonard, *Of Mice and Magic: A History of American Animated Cartoons*, McGraw Hill, New York, 1980

-- --, *The Disney Films*, Crown Publishers, Inc., New York; Thomas Nelson, London, 1973 (revised edition 1984)

Morgan, Louise, *Mickey's Future*, News Chronicle, 15 June 1935

Munsey, Cecil, *Disneyana; Walt Disney Collectibles*, Hawthorn Books, New York, 1974

Powell, Dilys, *Disney Profiles*, The Saturday Book, Hutchinson, London, 1943/The Best of the Saturday Book, Hutchinson, London, 1981

Schickel, Richard, *The Disney Version: The Life, Times, Art and Commerce of Walt Disney*, Simon & Schuster, New York; Weidenfeld & Nicholson, London, 1968

Seldes, Gilbert, *Mickey Mouse Maker*, The New Yorker, 19 December 1931

-- --, *No Art, Mr. Disney?*, Esquire, September 1937

Sendak, Maurice, *Growing Up With Mickey*, TV Guide, 11 November 1978

Shale, Richard, *Donald Duck Joins Up – The Walt Disney Studio during World War II*, UMI Research Press, Michigan, 1982

Silverstone, Murray, *Disney in 1935*, Picturegoer Weekly, 1935

Skolsky, Sydney, *Mickey Mouse – Meet your Maker*, Cosmopolitan, February 1934

Smith, David R., *Ub Iwerks, 1901-1971*, Funnyworld Magazine, 1972

-- --, *Fifty Years of Mickey Mouse Time*, Starlog Magazine, 1984

Taves, Isabella, *I Live With a Genius – a conversation with Mrs. Walt Disney*, McCall's Magazine, 1953

Taylor, Deems, *Walt Disney's Fantasia*, Simon & Shuster, New York, 1940

Theisen, Earl, *Sound Tricks of Mickey Mouse*, Modern Mechanix, January 1937

Thomas, Bob, *The Art of Animation*, Simon & Shuster, New York, 1958 (reprinted Golden Press, 1966)

-- --, *Walt Disney: An American Original*, Simon & Shuster, New York, 1976 (published in London by New English Library as *The Walt Disney Biography*)

Thomas, Frank and Johnston, Ollie, *Disney Animation – The Illusion of Life*, Abbeville Press, New York, 1981

Thompson, Don and Lupoff, Dick, *The Comic-Book Book*, Arlington House, New York, 1973

Tibbetts, John, *Of Mouse and Man*, American Classic Screen, May/June 1978

Wallace, Irving, *Mickey Mouse: And How He Grew*, Collier's, 9 April 1949

Mouse and Man, Time, 27 December 1937

Father Goose, Time, 27 December 1954

FILMOGRAPHY

1928
Steamboat Willie
Gallopin' Gaucho
Plane Crazy
The Barn Dance

1929
The Opry House
When the Cat's Away
The Barnyard Battle
The Plow Boy
The Karnival Kid
Mickey's Follies
Mickey's Choo-Choo
The Jazz Fool
Jungle Rhythm
The Haunted House
Wild Waves

1930
Just Mickey
The Barnyard Concert
The Cactus Kid
The Fire Fighters
The Shindig
The Chain Gang
The Gorilla Mystery
The Picnic
Pioneer Days

1931
The Birthday Party
Traffic Troubles
The Castaway
The Moose Hunt
The Delivery Boy
Mickey Steps Out
Blue Rhythm
Fishin' Around
The Barnyard Broadcast
The Beach Party
Mickey Cuts Up
Mickey's Orphans

1932
- *The Duck Hunt*
The Grocery Boy
The Mad Dog
Barnyard Olympics
Mickey's Revue
Musical Farmer
Mickey In Arabia
Mickey's Nightmare
Trader Mickey
The Whoopee Party
Touchdown Mickey
The Wayward Canary
The Klondike Kid
Mickey's Good Deed

1933
Building a Building
The Mad Doctor
Mickey's Pal Pluto
Mickey's Mellerdrammer
Ye Olden Days
The Mail Pilot
Mickey's Mechanical Man
Mickey's Gala Premiere
Puppy Love
The Steeple Chase
The Pet Store
Giantland

1934
Shanghaied
Camping Out
Playful Pluto
Gulliver Mickey
Mickey's Steam Roller
Orphans' Benefit
Mickey Plays Papa
The Dognapper
Two-Gun Mickey

1935
Mickey's Man Friday
The Band Concert (1st Mickey color)
Mickey's Service Station
Mickey's Kangeroo
Mickey's Garden
Mickey's Fire Brigade
Pluto's Judgment Day
On Ice

1936
Mickey's Polo Team
Orphans' Picnic
Mickey's Grand Opera
Thru the Mirror
Mickey's Rival
Moving Day
Alpine Climbers
Mickey's Circus
Mickey's Elephant

1937
The Worm Turns
Magician Mickey
Moose Hunters
Mickey's Amateurs
Hawaiian Holiday
Clock Cleaners
Lonesome Ghosts

1938
Boat Builders
Mickey's Trailer
The Whalers
Mickey's Parrot
Brave Little Tailor
The Fox Hunt (Donald Duck cartoon)

1939
Society Dog Show
The Pointer
Mickey's Surprise Party (for National Biscuit Co.)
The Standard Parade (for Standard Oil Co.)

1940
Tugboat Mickey
Pluto's Dream House
Mr. Mouse Takes a Trip
Fantasia ('The Sorcerer's Apprentice')

1941
The Little Whirlwind
The Nifty Nineties
Orphans' Benefit
A Gentleman's Gentleman (Pluto Cartoon)
Canine Caddy (Pluto Cartoon)
Lend a Paw (Pluto cartoon)

1942
Mickey's Birthday Party
Symphony Hour
All Together (For National Film Board of Canada)

1943
Pluto and the Armadillo (Pluto cartoon)

1946
Squatter's Rights (Pluto cartoon)

1947
Mickey's Delayed Date
Fun and Fancy Free ('Mickey and the Beanstalk')

1948
Mickey Down Under
Mickey and the Seal
Pluto's Purchase (Pluto cartoon)

1949
Pueblo Pluto (Pluto cartoon)

1950
Crazy Over Daisy (Donald Duck cartoon)

1951
Plutopia
R'coon Dawg

1952
Pluto's Party
Pluto's Christmas Tree

1953
The Simple Things

1983
Mickey's Christmas Carol